Around Leek

Memories of Leek & Nearby Villages

Compiled by Sheila Hine

Front Cover: Percy Goodall, Horton
Back Cover: New Street, early 1900s

CHURNET VALLEY BOOKS
1 King Street, Leek, Staffordshire. ST13 5NW 01538 399033 www.leekbooks.co.uk
© Sheila Hine and Churnet Valley Books 2013
ISBN 9781904546931

Leek Station with Gas Works behind.

A bargee at Cheddleton

BELOW:
Leek Station c. 1907

CONTENTS

Ashbourne Road early 1900s

ACKNOWLEDGEMENTS

Thanks to all the people who have contributed stories and photographs, also to the Leek Post and Times for the use of some photographs. Also to Geoff and Jean Fisher, and to Geoff Browne.

WALLGRANGE
ABOVE
Wallgrange Station,
Edwardian times

LEFT
Wallgrange 1952
Courtesy J. Morten

BELOW
Wallgrange Brickworks.
probably 1920s

Longsdon 1903

We came to Longsdon in May 1903 to a house in Sutherland Road. The front of the house faced over the fields away from the road and the back faced the road, on the other side of which was Mollatts Wood. Mollatt was the last keeper, before that it had been Hann's Wood. There was no keeper in our time; it was fairly extensive, part pine and part deciduous. Occasionally we saw red squirrels in the trees. Some years before the 1914 War the wood was sold along with Wall Grange Farm; it used to belong to the Duke of Sutherland. I heard that the farmer who bought it sold the timber from the wood during the war for as much as he paid for the whole estate.

When we came to Longsdon you could change the name of a house at will. I don't remember what our house was called but it didn't please us so my father chose the name 'Woodroyd' after a district in Yorkshire where his grandfather had lived. 'Royd' meaning field was a suitable name as the house was between the wood and fields. Two years later when we moved to a more convenient house we took the name with us and the name remained with that house also.

Another memory remains vividly in my mind. It was later in the year on a still warm night with the moon at the full. We sat at the sitting room window watching Mr Barber scything his field of hay. The shimmering moonlight illuminating the rhythmically moving figure, the swish of the scythe as it cut the grass and the scent of new mown hay - it was unforgettable.

In those days there were many smallholdings where the father of the family did some other work; Mr Barber was a shoemaker. Another man with a small farm was Mr Woolliscroft of Grove Cottage. He drove the local mail into Stoke each evening, put up there for the night and drove out with the morning mail. I think he left Longsdon about 6.30 each evening, picking up mail from other villages on the way to Stoke. Leaving Stoke in the early morning he delivered mail on the way out; Longsdon was the last village. I don't know what time he left Stoke but the letters were sorted and delivered and we got ours before my father left home to catch the 8.30 train to Stoke.

The mail for Leek was arranged separately. In the evening we used to see the van with two horses passing through the village about 8.30 pm and not stopping anywhere on the way. Later we had an afternoon delivery around the central triangle of the village, certainly during the 1914 War. The mail came out on a train leaving Stoke about 2.00pm. It was convenient that a letter posted in Stoke before 11.30 am would reach us before tea; there were advantages to the penny post!

In those days the railway station played an important part in the life of the village; the busiest time about 8.30am. Within 10 minutes of each other, a train went each way then. The train to Leek connected with a Churnet Valley train to Manchester. The train to Stoke connected with the London train. The business men travelled by those trains; they formed little groups, each sitting in their accustomed seats. The ones going to the Potteries were joined by another contingent from Endon.

Milk also travelled by those trains; at Wall Grange there would be 14 or 15 floats and at Endon about 30. At Stockton Brook where the station was below road level there was a special slope made for the milk churns. Some of the milk went to Manchester via Leek, some to London via Stoke. The farmers then collected their empty churns.

The next train to Leek arrived at Wall Grange about 10.20. Friends coming for a day in the country arrived by that train and it was the one we used for shopping in Leek. As a rule we came back from Leek by a train about 12.30 but in the case of urgent need it was possible to make a hurried dash up to town, do one shop and get a train back which left Leek for Stoke about 11.15. The snag was that in your anxiety not to miss the train you might arrive breathless at the station feeling you had not a minute to spare, see a train about to leave, hurl yourself onto it to find your first stop was Cheddleton station! A train for the Churnet Valley was due to leave a few minutes before the Stoke train and if late it might be leaving at the time scheduled for the Stoke train. I think most of us did that at least once; the long walk from Cheddleton Station taught us our lesson.

At one time a box of fish came to Wall Grange by the 10.20 train. Andrew Dawson from Cheddleton came with a cart, met the train and opened the box of fish outside the station and we came down to buy what we wanted before he set off for his Cheddleton round. Another way of getting fish was by having a standing order with a firm in Grimsby. There were two prices - for 2/6d you had a bag of white fish; whatever was plentiful - cod or haddock; or for 3/6d you had a bag which might include plaice or lemon sole. It was beautifully fresh, packed in a rush bag and delivered to the house.

The canals were much used in those days especially the lower canal. All the coal for the Cheddleton Paper Mills came by canal and the other way there were barges of stone from Cauldon Quarries that was sent down to the canal by chute to Froghall station. The barges were most picturesque; the cabins painted in pretty scenes often of castles and trees. The bargee's wife would often have a colourful shawl on her head and be sitting in the barge guiding the horse.

There were no motors then on the main road, I forget when I saw my first one but I do remember standing by the shop to watch General Booth of the Salvation Army being driven by car to Leek. He was standing in the car to wave to groups of people gathered to watch his progress. I think my brother had the first car in Longsdon in 1912.

The trades people all had their horse drawn vans; the doctors their light high traps or gigs. Then the farmers' carts and carts with coal etc so the road was fairly busy. On Wednesdays, Leek Market day, there were also droves of cattle being driven to market. Local cows were sometimes driven from field to field by road. At one time as I returned from posting in the evening I used to meet a Mrs Jolly driving cows home to be milked. I didn't know her and felt shy about greeting her. She was such a drab figure; I never remember a scrap of colour about her. At last I ventured a shy 'Good Evening' and was rewarded with one of the most beautiful smiles I have ever seen.

Another inhabitant who frightened me was old Mr Knight. My impression of him was of a very shaky old man with a white face and a lot of hair whose trembling hands looked quite unfit to control the spirited horse he rode. Knight's farm was one of the highest points in Longsdon and belonged to Trinity College, Cambridge, to be let at a small rent as long as there was a John Knight as a tenant. The last JK was the son of the old man and when he died the farm was sold.

The church was not built when we came to Longsdon but building started soon after. The school was a Church school and the first school master, a Mr Roberts, had started services there on the Sunday. He was a lay reader and Longsdon was in the parish of All Saints, Leek. By the time we came there was a resident 'curate-in-charge', Mr Warren, and we were still in All Saints parish, but when the church was consecrated in 1905 Longsdon was made a separate parish.

Sunday services were held in the school. During the week the chancel was screened off; on Sundays that was opened up and the desks were turned over to make backrests for the forms. It was uncomfortable for grown people but there was a big gap between the seat and the back. One of the incidents most Sundays was to see which of the Warren children would fall between. No doubt it made a bit of a change during the sermon. We wondered if they took it in turns!

Mr Lord the schoolmaster played the American organ. He played very efficiently for hymns and psalms and valiantly coped with a Voluntary before and after services. He only played two Voluntaries so we always had one of them twice each Sunday. His favourite was a gay tune - not very ecclesiastical - we usually had that at the end of the service.

Mr Turner, the Smith, had a very wide reputation and people brought their horses some distance. So there was often a horse being shod and perhaps another waiting when you passed.

Next to the Smithy was a pond and then Mr Plant's workshop. This was very convenient; sometimes you could see a cartwheel laid on the ground near the pond by Mr Plant, and Mr Turner bringing out the red-hot iron ring to be placed on its rim then water from the pond poured over to cool it.

Winifred Haigh 1970

Winifred Haigh and her 'invalid' vehicle in which she would often be seen travelling to Leek

The Gerald Horsley church consecrated in 1905

BELOW:
At Longsdon Church, pre-First World War.
Hermione Warren centre.

Mrs Warren

In 1879 the Leek Embroidery Society was established by Lady Elizabeth Wardle, wife of Sir Thomas, famous for silk dyeing in Leek. The Society was renowned nationally for the quality of their work, especially the ecclesiastical pieces, and in the 1880s for a complete, full-sized copy of the Bayeux tapestry.

Mrs Beatrice Ethel Warren was the wife of the Revd Warren, the first vicar of St Chad's at Longsdon. She was an accomplished artist and a distinguished member of the Society. Gerald Horsley was the architect for the church and he also designed the textiles within. A number of these dramatic compositions were stitched by Mrs Warren. She worked white, green and violet altar frontals, still used today, developing a characteristic method of stitching which complemented Horsley's work. The largest piece was a red frontal depicting the Annunciation for Zanzibar Cathedral where her son Revd Hugh St John P. Warren was the minister. She completed pieces for other churches including an angel in All Saints, Leek. She worked at home, as did many of the Society, and she continued to stitch at 3 Southfields in Leek almost until she died aged 89 in 1955.

(Information from Dr Brenda King, *Stitch and Stone: A History of Leek Embroidery Society* and *Dye, Print, Stitch: Textiles by Thomas and Elizabeth Wardle*.)

Mrs Warren, Hugh, Stephanie, Hermione and Rev. Percy.

Harry Foster

I was 9 when we flitted from Leek to Longsdon in 1932. At Longsdon School the boys had to play in the middle of the road because the bit of ground round the school was for the girls and they wouldn't have them playing together. Then Miss Haigh bought the field at the back for the lads to play in to get them off the road.

When I left school I did a bit o' farming; I worked for Clifford Buxton at Rudyard and Harold Keeling at Bradnop. I got half a crown a week and my keep and came home every Sunday, had my dinner, got a clean shirt and back again for the rest of the week.

When I was 18, I had my call-up papers and you had to go unless you worked on a farm and they got you off. Keelings' said to me, 'You've been a good youth; we want to keep you on and we've decided to give you a rise - sixpence a week. I said, 'You can keep it - I'm goin' - I've got a better job.' I didn't want farming; it wasn't in me.

When I'd done my training, I was sent to Folkestone; it was the first coastal defence. The pier had a concrete base with a Browning machine gun on. The bloke who was with me was named Fitzgerald and we did 2 hours on and 4 off. This 2 hours we went down and it was a lovely sunny day. We got comics out - reading *Dandy*. There were 2 planes coming, about 200 feet above the water towards us. We thought, 'These are our planes coming back.' They weren't; they were 2 Jerries. They flew round us and machine-gunned us. We opened fire but whether we hit 'em, I dunner know. They had me up the office over it. 'Did you hit them?' 'How can I tell? - we fired!' 'Oh, we can tell - we saw the tracer bullets.'

A month after, they gathered us all together and we went Portsmouth and they shut us in a great big pen - thousands of us - we didn't know what for, you couldn't write home. It was getting ready for D-Day.

We were dropped in 8-10 foot of water carrying your gun and pack on your back. You struggled out or you drowned - which a lot did. Me, at 5ft 2 could walk on the bottom. I swallowed a lot of sea water and didn't care whether they killed me or not - I were that sick. We had keep goin' because Jerry's shelling the beach and you're trampling over dead people. You were that terrified - you knowed you were goin' be killed, no doubt about it - shells droppin' all round you, half of 'em getting blown to bits, you were lucky or not.

There were only about a dozen left out of our regiment, the Kings Shropshire Light Infantry, if that; thousands were killed. It's in your head, your not going come back - that's it - end of the line. It drives you vacant but luck must have been on my side; I was only wounded on the head. When the shells explode, fine dust flies off 'em, all black speckles of explosion dust. Your head was peppered; your hat only covered so much and it flirted underneath. I had a big black patch for years and years; it gradually came out.

On the second day there's hundreds lying dead, the stinks vile and whether you wanted to or not you had to bury the dead because you may have been there a week and you couldn't afford any disease amongst the troops. We had to wrap 'em in a blanket and dig little holes, not so deep 'cus they dug 'em up again; I buried no end.

You had two men in a trench; they didn't have long trenches then. We took it in turn to fetch breakfast; the other one fetched dinner. My mate went fetch breakfast one day and never come back. When Sergeant Major came round to check if we were alright, he says, 'What you on your own for?' I said, 'He went fetch breakfast and never come back.' 'Oh, I'll see about it.' He came back after half an hour. 'When they were shelling, a piece of shell has gone through his wrist and he died of shock, the doctor says. We'll send you another man.' We were holed up at a Chateau-Ville-en-Vexin. We lost half a battalion there.

When you'd been so long in the line, they fetched you out for a rest to what they called a Echelon and they asked, 'Who can drive?' They wanted wagon drivers to supply the front line. They picked you out and you got a wagon and took supplies up. They called that a rest period! And if there were a lot of casualties and it was urgent - 'Who can drive?' and it's up to the front. I was infantry and just happened to become a driver. I had one rest from D-Day till we got to Minden in Germany. I came home and had 6 days. We were in Holland and I thought it would be finished when I got back; I were wrong!

I used cook chickens when they couldn't get food up to you if Jerry was shelling. Or rabbits - anything you could get hold of because where you'd come to they'd gone and you got everything as was left; that was if they was alive, half the animals were dead.

We carried on, hit and miss, all the way to Germany and then more and more Germans were packing up, coming down and holding their hands up. We found out when them big Tiger tanks made a put for us and shelled us. They stopped and come no farther; we didn't know why. They're 60 ton and were running out of fuel; they couldn't get juice to supply 'em and if we'd known, we'd got 'em trapped. They wanted enough to withdraw, they always pulled back to the high spots. If they hadn't, they'd a left tanks for us. They were clever.

When we crossed the Rhine, people were good to us. They were ordinary people; they didn't want the war. Half of 'em were living under hedges and bridges; their houses had been bombed and shattered.

When the war finished, I was in Minden in Germany, then trouble broke out between the Jews and the Arabs in Palestine and they sent troops there to keep them apart and I was one of them. We had tents outside the Palestine Police barracks. There was a regiment of us - the KSLI and we had to patrol the city.

We'd been outside the barracks for about 2 weeks and on a Sunday morning there came a Padre round. This day he came and called 'Church' and the men started waking up. I looked up and thought, 'This is funny.' I was looking up at the sky, the tent had gone. I looked round and the other soldiers were doing the same, looking round.

There were 8 big tents gone, with 24 under a tent. The Arabs had pinched them while we were asleep. There were guards on and 'Dannert wire', rolls and rolls round the compound about 20 foot high, but they'd got over. It was thought they came with a couple of camels and threw some rugs over the wire to pull it down. They'd sell them to the Arabs out in the desert - they'd pay a lot of money for them; all the tribes in the desert used tents. They never caught 'em. We couldn't understand how no-one had heard anything; I daresay we'd had a drink or two.

Another time we were out on parade. You had to roll your tent up half way so air could go through and all your blankets were rolled up and put at the top of your bed in a pile with your pillow. Then you'd go out on parade and while we were there one of these Arabs would come round selling oranges. He rode on a donkey with big baskets of oranges on either side. Then he used to shift these oranges out and pinch the blankets off our beds - we couldn't get to him because we were on parade. Then he used put these oranges back on top of the blankets and off he went, round the camp and out.

When we come off parade we went after him in a truck and as we caught up with him we drove past with a big stick out and knocked him off the donkey into the road. He never came for any more blankets. It was the job of the Palestine Police to get them back. We daren't tell 'em what we'd done else they'd a had us in jail.

We stayed just over 6 months then they moved us to Cyprus for a rest period and that's where I was demobbed. They offered to make me up to a sergeant but I said I'd seen enough. I had £100 and a suit for 5 years service.

The Leek Brook and Leekbrook railway bridge.

Joshua Wardle's works at Leekbrook c.1920s.

Gladys Sutton

I was born in July 1917. My father was Joshua Mayer Victor Steele and for a while we lived on a smallholding at Leekbrook. He had worked for a baker on Sheepmarket driving the horses, and he took visitors to Buxton with horses and coach. He always liked horses; he'd rather have them than cattle. When we farmed at Basford he was good at vetting and shod our own horses and some for our neighbours. He'd bring the shoes into the house and put them in the fire, then go outside and hammer them into shape. But mother would say 'horses won't fill the milk churn.'

My mother Ethel came from a big family, the Gerrards from Hulland. They were farmers and cattle dealers and used to go to market two or three times a week to Ashbourne or Derby with pony and governess cart.

She was a personal maid to Lady Shrewsbury at Alton Towers and went to France with her. She had to sort all her clothes out and help her. She was a teenager and had an 18 inch waist. I think Aunty Bess lived and worked at Alton Towers and she

Ethel (Mum) with Granny & Grandad Gerrard.

got mother the job. Lady Shrewsbury said 'Would you like to work with me?' so she stayed a number of years. I always remember her telling us that she was once putting shoes onto her Ladyship's feet and caught her toe. Lady Shrewsbury took her shoe off and was going to hit mother but mother said 'Your Ladyship if you do that, I will do the same to you.' And soon after I think she left.

Aunt Bess said that when the servants knew they were coming back down the long drive they would all scuttle round. 'Her Ladyship's coming!' I think they were frightened of her. Mother said Lady Shrewsbury's ceiling was embossed in gold with E for Elizabeth.

At Leekbrook it was a bungalow with ground near the old cottages going to the railway. Dad had a cowshed at Little Birchall where he had kept cows and milked them when he had lived on Junction road. I remember the bungalow and you went under the bridge and up the field where there was a pigsty and hills each side and over the hill was the golf links. He had mowing grass over the railway; it was busy there then. There were goods wagons and behind us the railway went up to Cauldon and

Ethel Gerrard in France

Waterhouses and when the trains went past the drivers used to wave to us. The road was very quiet.

There were cottages on the road from the bridge to Basford; I suppose the people worked at Wardles. The Wardle family lived at the big house; they were the bosses. Near to the Cenotaph there were four cottages and the end one was Mrs Renshaw's shop - they were all related in the row. Past there was a big detached house and the road up to Wardle's house which you can't use now.

There were the railway cottages and then four bungalows and beyond that, four more. Years ago they'd no fresh water there and you used to go up to one of the houses where Fleets lived to fetch drinking water. I knew all of them. Great big iron gates led to these railway cottages and there was a brook at the bottom from where we fetched water to fill the boiler, then a field and a stream and then Wardle's works. You could see the people at the back and then they built the new works. A lot of local people worked there and on the railway; it was a busy place. The fathers or husbands worked on the railway and the rest of the family at Wardles.

Mother used to put tassles on silk scarves and they used to deliver them in cases. I always remember she used to have them on the table with a heavy thing to hold them down and she used to put these fringes on. They had silk scarves in them days. Then, when she'd done so many, after so many days, they had to go back.

She once had some painters lodging and a young fellow came who worked at the new works. He was Scottish and stayed many years. Wardles also manufactured a lot of stockings and then in the new works in one department they did screen printing.

We moved to the Sneyd Arms at Basford when I was 12. We went to look at it on the horse and cart. I said 'We aren't coming to live here are we?' it did look a dump. There was some jam above the fireplace on the mantelpiece and some pewter which was left from it being a pub many years before. We hardly dare go up some stairs because it was in such a state. There was a big room - some hard work up there I'll tell you, no water and no electric, two landings, a cold place in winter. If people were hiking past and the door was open they'd walk in, thinking it was still a pub so mother did a bit of catering - if anyone wanted a cup of tea she'd get tea for them and go in the pantry and make up a few fresh scones.

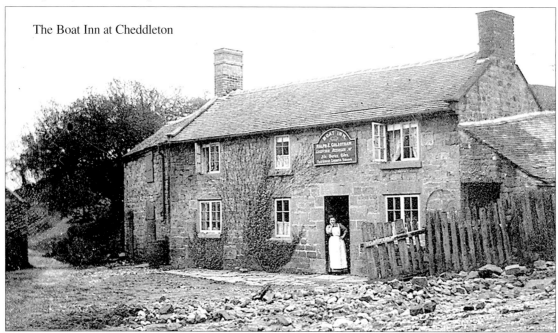

The Boat Inn at Cheddleton

Mum with friends at the
Sneyd Arms

Mum and Clifford
in the centre of picture

BELOW:
Mosslee Hall Farm, Basford

There were 70 acres there rented from the Sneyd family. I remember milking; the milk had to be taken down to Cheddleton where it was picked up on the main road near the Churnet Bridge. Eventually the wagon came up to Basford and the farm below brought their milk up to the Smithy.

Gladys on horse with her Mum, Ethel.

I remember setting and picking potatoes; we'd take them to the golf links to sell at 12/6 a hundredweight and if I went blackberrying we used to take a basket and I'd get a bob or two.

I remember being in the hayfield and the cornfield. We had once loaded a cart with hay and going downhill it all slid off. Father said 'Get on and load it again.' I said 'No.' So my sister got on and it did it again. It was so short it wouldn't grip together. We used to be in the hayfield when people were going past to Ipstones Show and I used to say 'Can we go?' and he'd say 'No, You're in this hayfield.'

Miss Clowes's farm was opposite the Sneyd Arms; it was the Smithy when we went there - Jim Ousley was blacksmith and lived in the cottage and Clowes's were joiners and builders. About six worked there.

Keelings were at Mosslee Mill for many years; a nice family. He worked down at Froghall and Mrs Keeling used to see to the cattle. He worked down there because the farm wouldn't keep them; it's very banky.

Lewis's had the Lodge Farm; it all belonged to the Sneyd Family, well, Mrs Dugdale as she was then. I used to take the milk every morning in a little can to Basford Hall. There was a staff of 3; a butler, a cook and a parlour maid and then they had a gardener, Mr Lees. Occasionally if they had a dance we used to go up and sneak a look through a window to see them dancing round in their finery. Mrs Dugdale came to pay the milk bill perhaps once a month. She was a very refined lady. They had one daughter; I remember she used to ride a pony and it bolted and threw her off up the drive and they came to our place and said to dad 'Can you do anything; the horse has thrown Avril.' And they found it down by the canal bridge at Cheddleton. Avril was very nice; when I took the milk, she'd be grooming and feeding the horses then come into the kitchen where the cook was and cut some bread - she'd no idea; it was very thick slices. They were good landlords.

We had to use the train on Saturdays to go shopping in Leek, walking up into town from the station. I used to say 'Come on Mother, train's coming.' You could hear it coming from Consall. When the driver saw us near the weighbridge, he'd put his hand up and we had to get our ticket, cross over and get on the train, but he never left us; we were always last minute.

My sister Doris worked in Leek at Tattons on a machine, then they moved to Mayfield and wanted her to go because she was such a good worker but mother said 'No, it's too far to go.' Mother used to take her to Leekbrook on the saddle of the bike to catch a bus - mother pedalled.

The boats on the canal took coal to Brittains. Their name was Firkins - I can remember them because they had their families on with them. The woman used to guide the boat and the man would have the pony. Then they went onto Consall and picked up something to take back to the Potteries.

I used to go to Cheddleton Church with Edith Brassington from next door at Basford Hall Farm most Sunday nights and we'd go to Churnet Hall dancing and they had sewing, needlework,

Leek Railway Station Goods Yard early 20th century.

Basford Hall c.1910

Cheddleton Wharf, with off-loaded bricks from Wallgrange, probably on the way up to the site of the new Cheddleton Asylum, completed in 1897.

leatherwork and cookery lessons there too. Once there was a dance at Bradnop so we went with Gladys Fernihough from Yew Tree Farm. We went past Eardley's at Finney Lane and came out at Ashenhurst. Coming back I stopped the night at Yew Tree Farm.

When I worked at Brittains I had to go for 6am. I worked in the sorting shed, sorting raw materials to see if there was rubber in it because it spoiled the paper; it was dusty like sawdust. Then in another department it was wet materials. I met my husband Archie; most of his family worked there, well a lot of local people did. They were nice people to work for but like everywhere else the pay was only about half a crown an hour. You did get a bit of a bonus about every 12 months, you were lucky to get £5 a week. I used to work 6 till 4 and if they were busy Mr Day used to say 'Can you work over for an hour?' and I used to think 'Well, its half a crown.' I had a money box from Leek and Moorlands Building Society and what I'd got I put in and when it was full of 2 shillings and half crowns, take it and have it emptied. I think when I left and got married in 1942 I'd got about £70.

I was at Basford sitting in a chair and at the corner by the grate was a little shelf with a wireless on it and I remember Mr Chamberlain saying war was declared. He'd got a deep, soulful voice and I thought 'Oh dear!' There were so many local lads called up - a lot as I knew. Archie's brother went through Dunkirk and came back. He was digging trenches in Southampton when it fell in on him and by the time they got him out he'd gone. He was 22.

Archie went into the Infantry and when he told me I went mad. He had a rough time out in Italy and Greece. He got wounded but came home safe. It was all very sad.

In the Leek Post and Times, June 1953 it was reported that a 1770 coach believed to be one of the oldest of its kind in the country had been given an airing. It was taken along the lanes and roads of Cheddleton much the same as it had done 100 years previously when it was the conveyance of the Sneyd family of Basford Hall. The two horses were lent by Mr V Steele who also occupied the driver's seat. Riding inside were Mr T Brassington and Mr W Steadman of the Basford Bridge Carnival Committee who stopped to make collections for British Empire Cancer Research. Mr L Steadman was in attendance as footman. The coach was lent by trustees of Mr JW Sneyd's estates.

CHEDDLETON SCHOOL 1930S
The names entered here were supplied by Anne Hedley, long time teacher.
Teachers' names were not included.

Back L-R: Francis Leese, Alan Johnson, Bernard Alcock, John Taylor, Fred Sutton, Bill Hammond, Bill Connor,
Albert Plant, -- Vernon?, Sid Pickford, Victor Martin, Geoffrey Morton, Bill Bunn, -- Bullock?, -- Whittaker?
Kneeling: Ernest Hough, Derek Turner, Harry Pegg, Ron Brown, Laurence Clowes, Graham Spooner, Ken Brown. --,
Donald Sutton, Harold Berresford, Eric Johnson, --, --, Ernest Clowes.

Back Row: Grace Fisher, Ken Oliver, Muriel Crofts, Philip Clowes, Hilda Wain, Alan Pegg, Margaret Massey, Clifford Blakeman, Louie Goodwin,
Seated: Nancy Hood, --- Birley, Roy Gilbert, John Cordon, Oswald Eardley, Horace Speed, -- Eardley?
Front: Dennis Fernyhough, Ken Findler, -- Turner, Ken Kent.

Back: Mrs Wilde, Ken Kent, Harold Lomas, Basil Bagshaw, Alan Pegg, Fred Wilshaw, Peter Renshaw, George Evans.
Mid: Margaret Steele, M. Fellows?, Betty Coladine, Muriel Crofts, Barbara Hewitt, Barbara Scott, Betty Birley, Ken Ollerhead
Front: Dennis Fernyhough, Ken Findler, Raymond Gyte, Ivy Wilkes, Clive Barker, Oswald Eardley.

Back: Sylvia Wallace, Evelyn Mellor, Sylvia Spooner, Jessie Renshaw, Evelyn Fisher, Marjorie Barker, Hilda Bloor,
Betty Stubbs, Irene Dawson, Irene Alcock, Muriel Eason, Nellie Turner.
Middle: Alan Johnson,.Ada Price, Brenda Lane (Arrowsmith), Gladys Renshaw, Vera Bagshaw, Kathleen Blakeman,
Clarice Alcock, Mary Priestman, Eva Hammersley, Connie Heath, Gladys Steele, Fred Sutton
Front: Francis Leese, Bernard Alcock, Bill Connor, Vernon -, John Taylor, Sid Pickford, Norman or Stan Staton, Billy Bunn, --

Back: Jack Wilshaw, Roy Chell, Jock Bunn, Norman Staton, Eric Keeling, Gordon Stanley, Lance? Eardley,
Alfred Burndred, John Barlow.
Mid: Beattie Finney, Vera Morris, Eileen Wheawall, Ena Goodwin, Muriel Spooner, Freda Keeling, Eva Turner,
Hilda Stanton, Ida Pearson, Sidney Forrester, Meryl Gilbert, Ada Wilkes, Iris Fernyhough, Dorothy Faulkner.
Kneeling: John Cordon, Doug Renshaw, Harry Starling, --, Barbara Birch, Clifford Steele, Peter Birch, Bernard Salt
Sat: Arthur Evans, Roger Turner, Peter Hedley, Tom Finney, Malcolm Findler, Gordon Alcock, Derek Hill, --, Douglas Bowyer

Back L-R: Derek Bateman, Eric Keeling, Arthur Clowes
Middle: Jack Bunn, Arthur Evans, Roy Holland, Les Bateman, Stanley Kirkham, Tom Finney
Seated: Roger Turner, Lionel Alcock, Derek Hill, -- Birch, Gordon Alcock

Back: Derek Turner, Graham Spooner, --, Victor Martin, Eva Hammersley, Harold Berresford, --, Bill Hammond,
Kathleen Braddock, Albert Plant.
Seated: Eva Alcock, Donald Sutton, Mary Wain, Ernest Hough, Mabel Baker, --, Freda Brookes, --.
Front: Bill Tait, -- Price, Laurence Clowes, Alice Finney, Geoffrey Moreton, Emily Dainty, Ron Brown.

Geoff Buxton

Uncle Nathan Buxton took the tenancy of Rudyard Hall in 1906 and left in 1927. He bought it when it was offered for sale in 1919; it was over 400 acres. He sold all the rough land off to Chawners; there wasn't much land there - it was only a hunting lodge to Fairboroughs.

John Wain came in 1927 and bought it and farmed it until 1939 when he died suddenly so they had a farm sale. Mother walked us up the lane and the field was full of black cars, no other colours, just black cars. Not many people had cars, they must have come from miles; he was a very well known bloke.

Mr and Mrs Dale then rented the farm from the Wain family. Mother used to collect for Dr Barnados and she'd walk up to Rudyard Hall with a lantern. They'd say 'Stop and have a bit of tea.' She'd only manage one place a night. Swindells another night, Wheeldons another.

Rudyard Chapel is now 100 years old, being built in 1912. When it was built Uncle

Rudyard, the Old Chapel.

Nathan bought a writing desk with a stool; a big thing and Aunt Maude said 'Nathan, whatever have you bought?' he said 'I can do my writing on it but if you don't like it that much, I'll give it to the chapel; they haven't got a pulpit.' And that is the pulpit in the chapel; Uncle Nathan's writing desk from Rudyard Hall. Before the first chapel was built in 1862 they used to have the services there at Rudyard Hall because this was Rudyard and where the chapel is now, was Harpers Gate; there were only a few houses there in the early 1800s.

Thomas William Buxton, my granddad was at Rudyard Green. Like all farmers they had to live off the land; they had plenty of rabbits. So he says to me granny, 'I'll just go see Nathan today.' He thought he'd get out of the rabbits. So he walked up to Uncle Nathan's. 'Ee Will', he says, 'I'm glad you've come, I've got a lovely rabbit for dinner.'

Granddad was there for 43 years, from 1916 to 1949. They tried to change the name to Rudyard Manor at one time. It was two miles from one end to the other, about 270 acres. It was a very good farm - what Jack Smith called a one horse farm. That was where one horse could pull a load all round the farm.

The Swindells family were at Pool End. They were all born at the Three Horseshoes on Blackshaw Moor; it was a pub and farm. They came to Pool End around the time of the First War. The young women went working in mills, Bob stayed at home and Tommy went labouring; there were 7 of them. Sam was the Black Sheep because he got married - the other 6 didn't.

I never knew the father but I knew Mother. She used to sit on a chair and they waited on her like a queen - what she said was law. She was about 86 when she died in 1957 and I was a bearer and they would have her die at home upstairs. They had put her in her coffin and to get it down the stairs, you never saw nothing like it. We had to stand it up straight to get it round a bend.

Mr & Mrs Robert Swindells.

RIGHT: Sam, Mary, Nelly, Bob,
Tom, Lily.

I had to teach Bob to drive a tractor - a 51 year old man who had never done anything only with a horse or bike. To get him to master the clutch was a work of art, you didn't have stand in front of him! But he got the hang of it and did ever so well with a little Fergy tractor.

They had a little black and white striped stall by the road; 2 of the sisters ran it. It was painted a horrible green later. The school bus would drop us off there - 16 children - and we'd have an odd penny so we used to call. They had pop, sweets, cigarettes and we'd jump up and sit on the counter and tell 'em we'd only got a penny and we wanted some caramels and they offered to give us 6 for a penny. We said 'But Mrs Pointon next door will give us 7 - she also sold sweets, pop and cigarettes in a little kitchen. 'No, no, we can't afford.' So we said we'd go see Mrs Pointon. 'No, we'll give you 7.' We used plague life out of 'em. They used open on a Sunday, lift the front up. They kept all this stuff but it was never broken into, different days then.

Robert Swindells with two of his children at the Three Horseshoes, Blackshaw Moor, where he was a farmer and licensed victualler.

Oakfields at Pool End
c.1920s

Left, Nelly

Below, a visitor to the
farm where they sold
refreshments. 1930s

At Willgate, Rudyard. Thought to be Sigleys horses.

Bob seen above and right

AT RUDYARD 1919

Top: The Green Farm

Middle:
Packsaddle Cottage

Below: Green Tree Farm

RUDYARD HALL
1919.

John Wain had started farming on his own at Lower House, Ferny Hill as a tenant and in 1913 moved to Throwley where he bought 1250 acres including the hall when it was sold in 1920. In 1927 he purchased Rudyard Hall and made it into a model farm including a Scandinavian type fattening house for 240 bacon pigs which was one of the first. He was president of the NFU in 1935 and took a leading role in the formation of the Milk Marketing Board and was NFU representative at the Empire Producers conference in Australia in 1938. He was a local preacher in the Mount Methodist Circuit for 30 years and died suddenly in 1939 after tragically losing his wife in 1937 from septicaemia and his daughter in 1938 in childbirth. SH

Alan Williamson

Around 1929-1930 my father-in-law, Charles Holdcroft was working for John Wain at Rudyard Hall. At that time they were milking over 90 cattle and retailing the milk in Leek. There were two girls each with a horse drawn conveyance; the milk was bottled and taken round the town. At that time it was still milking by hand; there were 8 of them and they milked 12 a piece and if anyone was missing, John Wain himself milked 12 although he was a senior man in the NFU, chairman at Leek, the county and eventually National President too. But he'd still settle down and milk 12 cows night and morning if there was a man ill or off for any reason. He could do anything - work horses or the like but of course when he was gone the men had to get on with it.

At the time Charles was there they had the first milking machine put in - the first one in the Staffordshire Moorlands. Blakemore and Chell put it in with a big diesel engine and milking machine pump. Then half of the men could manage; it took about 4 to keep the units going. This same engine charged batteries and made electricity for lighting purposes and also used to pump water. During that time there was never a tractor; it was all done with horses although there was a small machine with an engine on which pushed the muck out of the sheds.

JW would go off to London for several days at a time and it wasn't unusual for him to come back on the train late afternoon and walk back from the station - but if something wanted doing he'd be straight back to farm work. Charles couldn't speak highly enough of him and that he died so young was a great loss. When he was the President and bound by the rules to step down after his stint in office there was regret that a man so capable should have to. He travelled on one occasion to study milk production methods and marketing in New Zealand; he was very progressive, leading the way.

At one time he farmed Throwley Hall as a grazing farm and kept a lot of cattle up there all summer. Charles described how everybody but himself had to go and fetch these cattle back in October one year. They were driven all the way back by Waterhouses, Winkhill, Bradnop and through Leek to Rudyard Hall; a big bunch of cattle. Of course they were gone longer than expected, perhaps one or two got away and they would have to be gathered. Charles had instructions to set to milking soon after dinner and he was still milking at 8 o'clock when they came back. He'd done three quarters of them; they helped him finish off - he remembered that well.

Rudyard Hall 1919

Rudyard hockey girls
early 1920s.

RUDYARD JUBILEE QUEEN
MID 1930S

Left: Doris Machin on the right.

BELOW:
Charlie Haywood, the Policeman.
Forward girls. Left, Betty Bowcock,
Joyce Hooley, --, --, Barbara Hine.

Amy Hewitt

I was a dairy maid for Mr and Mrs Dale at Rudyard Hall. Mr Dale and my dad were both local preachers and were talking one day. Mr Dale said, 'I'm having a bit of trouble with my staff; the girls have these boyfriends and they will bring them back and they're smoking in the barns. I'm ever so worried lest they set the place on fire.' I was 16 so I think my dad offered me to go there and he sacked some of them.

I shared a room with Dora Bratt; we did housework - ironing and stuff - and helped in the fields and bottled the milk. The men used to milk by machine and carry the milk up to the dairy and tip it in a tank on top of the bottling stand. When we'd filled the bottles we put the tops on; it took quite a while. The Boss used to go round with a churn and a gill measure in a van as well as the crates of bottles. I went with him; we did several streets in Leek and a bit in Rudyard on the way. When we got back we had dinner, then had to wash the bottles by hand. That was a bit dicey if you broke one. There was a tank of soapy water and a brush that came out, going round and you had to put the bottles on. Mrs Edge who worked there once cut her hand bad because she broke a bottle in the tank.

They advertised for a lad and Bob came from Halifax. Fred Robinson was a local cattle dealer who went to York Market - that's where he saw Bob looking for a job. He said, 'I know where there's a job going but it's miles away in Staffordshire.' He got the job, tractor driver and all sorts. He was a town lad but had worked on a couple of farms. There was also Arthur Machin and Cliff Edwards working there.

I enjoyed my time at Rudyard Hall; Bob and I went out together - I used to iron for 5 people but never did Bob's; he took his washing home to Halifax! We got married and he wanted a farm of his own so we bought Triangle Farm and some stock but we might have been better carrying on working; it would have been easier if we'd had some wages coming in and built up slowly.

We milked in the teens of cows. You had to have your buildings examined for a licence and there was a new building next to the house so when the inspector came we showed him this new building. It was lovely and clean but with no cow chains - they didn't detect there were no cows coming in there and passed it. The buildings where we had the cows, they didn't even look at that.

We stayed there for nine and a half years; our three children were born and reared there. It was a bleak place; if it snowed badly we could be blocked in for weeks. We had a big mortgage and when we sold it we didn't have much left. We moved to Herefordshire.

Mr & Mrs Charles Dale

Arthur Machin, 1930s

Arthur Machin at
Rudyard Hall 1930s

Below:
Joyce Heath, later
Buxton, working at
Rudyard Hall

Bob, Amy, Angela
and Peter

At Triangle Farm early 1950s

More from Triangle Farm early 1950s

Helping at Swainsmoor Aug 1965.
Maurice Parker, Philip Dale, Sheila & Angela Hewitt

Amy & Florrie Dale (mum)

Alice Bates

I was born at Naychurch in 1916. Me mam was Susan Mellor from Ladyrock and dad, David Mycock from Ipstones. They rented the farm from the Crewe and Harpur Estate. We had old fashioned oil lamps and a coal fire with a big ess-hole. It was a very happy home.

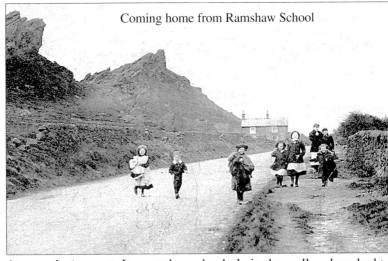

Coming home from Ramshaw School

Dad worked on the road, chopping stones in them days, as well as on the farm. There were 20 odd cows in a big shippon; we had to mex'n 'em out. It went through a hole in the wall and we had to do some hand-milking, sitting on a stool. We made butter in a great big churn and when it were thundery it wouldner turn - we were churnin' for hours. Any of us as were at liberty that was the job. We had to carry all the water from a trough for everything and fill a big furnace in the kitchen.

We used do a lot of climbing on the Rocks and I remember Roches Hall. The Brocklehursts had a party for all the children round at Christmas. Old Annie Parker used to be the gaffer there. It was lovely, games and all that, and the yaks, llamas and wallabies were in the field roaming about.

Dad, David Mycock c.1950

Dad used to get up at half past four in a morning to mow with a scythe all round the sides of the fields then somebody came to mow the rest for us. We all used have to rake and ted in the hayfield, all by hand, then make it into heaps and load it onto the cart. We put it on a loft and tread it down. Talk about dust!

We used go Ramshaw School, about 'afe a dozen at a time and carry a basket in turns with six dinners in. Mr and Mrs Davenport were teachers, very strict but very good - made you learn. There was a big old stove in the middle of room. When I left at 14 I cried 'cus I didner want leave. I worked at Tattons Mill till I were 26.

Ada, Fred
Mary, Alice, Hannah
Wilf

Ramshaw School early 1930s
Back: Eric Bratt, Raymond Grindey, Donald Thomson, Ken Ryder, Charlie Wain, John Bradley
Second: Fanny Mycock, Lucy Frodsham, Muriel Ryder, Amy Dale, Dora Bratt
Front: Frank Wain, Donald Clowes, Frank Frodsham, Violet Whittaker, Myrtle Dale, Clarence Stonier

Ramshaw School early 1920s
2nd row down: 2 Mary Mycock, 5 Ada Mycock, 6 Annie, 7 Minnie Warrington, 8 Emma Mellor
Third Row: 4 Alice Mycock, 7 Hannah Mycock
Fourth Row: 8 Wilfred Mycock, 9 Jack Warrington.   Front: Fred Mycock

It was Upperhulme Chapel, morning, noon and night on a Sunday for most of us; mum and dad only went on special occasions. We sang on stage at the Anniversary. It was bed at 9, we never went out till we were grown up then used go dancing at Warslow. Arthur Belfield lived at Strines and he had a taxi, a very old one, and we went with him but we had to be in by 11. Me mam never went bed till we got in, me dad never bothered. I loved it at Naychurch. Dad was guttering and fell and hurt his head, a bad accident. He died and mum gave the farm up.

My job at the mill was winding; it was the stuff as came into the mill, loads of it. You had to part the skeins and put 'em on this thing with about 20 bobbins on each side. If you had good work you went like mad and if you had bad work you couldn't get your living. We had a lot of laughs, the girls. Isaac Birch was our gaffer and if you didn't work you got cossed. Max Tatton was the boss - very smart; he used come round and look what you were doing, was we comfortable, any problems?

Hines kept a shop. Mrs Hine was a tall woman and used to do a lot of baking. When we came down the fields to work there was a winder at the back of the house and all this baking was in the winder - we used look at it. Nora and Nelly used to work in the shop and old Tommy used to keep the corn end.

When the war was on we used do night shifts, with a tin hat in case of bombs. When the planes came Mam would shout 'Come on, come on, there's a plane coming over - get in this pantry,' and we used run in and hide in case it bombed.

When I was young, I had rheumatic fever and I had to learn to walk again, I was so ill I was in bed a long time. I left work - you were called up. I wanted to go in the Land Army with my mate. We had to go to the doctors for an examination. Of course with having rheumatic fever it had left me with a weak heart so the doctor said I couldn't go in the Land Army or anything. So I said 'I'll go in the NAAFI.' He said 'If you do, it's your responsibility, if anything happens, you've volunteered.' So I went in the NAAFI, to Hixon, near Stafford. The army were there and we catered for them. That was where I met my husband; he was from a nearby farm.

There were Petty France cottages at the back of the old church in Leek and my sister Ada said there was one for sale when I came home. There'd been an old woman in, Mrs Ryder, she didn't tell us about the cockroaches. We went, it was Oakes Ash selling, it looked alright, one bedroom and an attic, a little kitchen - nice. So we thought we'd come back to Leek. Eric agreed. It cost £250 in 1954.

We hadn't been there long, it wanted a new grate. Frank Salt, he put grates in. He knocked the old one down - the mantelpiece was high - and all these cockroaches came out. Oh my goodness! He says 'Until you get rid of them, I'm coming nowhere near to put a grate in.' So we had to go to the Health Department for them to get rid of these cockroaches. I stayed with Ada and my husband went back to his parents. He thought I'd left him. The cottages have all gone now, Mr Rowbotham was the Health visitor in them days and he said 'These houses have got to come down; where would you like to go - Westwood or behind the Flying Horse?' There were 4 houses there then and that's where we went and Eric got on at Brittains Paper Mill.

We had a chip shop on St Edward Street. Ada bought it, well she rented it first. We worked together from then on. We had a 'dolly', like a churn and it worked with electric and we did the potatoes in it after the shop had closed. We had eye hole 'em with a peeler then we had a bath which we put 'em in with water and in them days there was a little secret, a little bit of liquid white to keep the taters fresh so they wouldner go brown.

Next morning Ada'd go across and drain 'em then we used to wipe 'em over before we could use 'em. I used go early and get all me papers ready, tissues and chipper. Then Ada used to cut the fish up and I used put the peas on the gas and used stand there so they wouldn't boil too quickly - simmer 'em and the minute they came up, switch it off otherwise they'd be all skinned. You had to stand there you see till they were done then you could switch it off and leave 'em. Then we would get everything organised because you can't do anything once the doors open.

Ada bought the chipper and the range from Mr Haworth when they retired from top of town,White Hart. There were 3 parts; you did chips in one, fish in another - you didn't have mix 'em. We used Frytick not dripping, we used have a traveller. It was a bit expensive but good stuff. We had drain it out every other day.

We opened up at half past 10 and away they'd come till half past 2. Then all to clean up; of course everything had to be wiped down, pans to be drained and clean the fan. We didn't open Sunday or Monday; you couldn't get fresh fish Mondays. Closed Thursday but we did Friday and Saturday nights till midnight. There used to be Bingo at the Palace Cinema. You ought to have seen them come in Saturday night when Bingo had finished. Eeh, crowds and crowds; there was only me and Ada but we managed. Ada'd do a lot of frying and I'd do a lot of serving. It was happy, it was lovely; we had some laughs, me and Ada. We used have 2 forms in and on a Wednesday the farmers came in. They used sit and talk; all these old farmers from Warsler and Elkstones - they've all gone.

Fish, chips and peas and made a good living. Fish came from Harry Pakeman in Fountain Street. He delivered it, just cod. You mixed your batter the night before, flour, water and a pinch of bicarb in a big bowl and covered it up - it's no use fresh. The peas came in a big bag, dried peas; we used soak 'em overnight.

I'd run to work 'cus I'd got two lads to look after, used organise the meals before I went, to come back to. Ada's husband, Ken used to come occasionally to help chip 'cus it was a hand chipper. He had a bowl under the chipper and this time he knocked it and they all fell off, all over the floor. He cossed; well, I couldner stop laughing and that made him worse so he went; he didn't do any more. They had to go in the bin and we had to do some more quick.

She bought the till from Haworths. It had got the prices on but it didn't register the right prices, you just had to press it to open it. There was a girl lived down Daisy Bank and she said

'Alice, I think you've overcharged me.' It registered more than I served her with so I shouted 'Ada, can you come a minute.' She says 'What's up?' I said 'this lady says I've overcharged her.' So Ada had to explain that all the reckoning was done in our heads. I wonder what they'd do now, all these supermarkets, if it wasn't all done for 'em.

We never had no bother - everybody was so good. We finished in 1988.

Mum (Susan).

The Hine girls from Dain's Mill, Upperhulme.

Nether Hay, Upperhulme

Under the Roches

Choir at Meerbrook
?1930s.

Below:
Garden Party at
Meerbrook Vicarage,
? 1920s.

Fanny Earl

I was the youngest of 14 born at Naychurch but 4 boys died in infancy, diphtheria and that sort of thing. My eldest sister Annie was a cripple and went to live with Aunty Anna down Mill Street because that was easier for her than being on the farm. Then there was Ada who went into service at Meerbrook with Cissie Hine's family at Wetwood. Fred went into service farming at Rushton; Mary, Hannah and Alice went to Tattons Mill in Upperhulme. Wilf went farming then there was Gladys, Jane and me.

**Early 1930s
Jane, Gladys
Fanny**

Dad worked for the council on the roads, breaking stone. He had to put bags round his legs. Spreading tar was very hard work too. He worked from Blackshaw Moor all the way to Flash so as he wasn't at home in the daytime, as each child grew up they did their bit on the farm until they left home. It was very hard work, all horse or hand work. Mother was a very strong woman too. We were brought up tough but you accepted that's how it was.

We had hens, pigs, milk cows and a horse. I didn't milk myself; dad would say I'd send the cows dry. Long before my time Mother used to go to Leek market with the horse and trap taking butter and eggs to sell and I remember her saying at one time she couldn't get tuppence a pound for the butter and had to bring it home.

In 1947 when the big snow came we used to have to dig through 6 foot snowdrifts to get the cows to the water trough but then when it got too bad and they couldn't get out we had to get snow and melt it in the boiler in the kitchen - we had a furnace - for the cattle to drink.

I remember working very hard at haymaking. At 5am dad used to whistle the horse and it came from what seemed miles off. And ploughing during wartime in a field across the main road and dad saying in a not very polite manner that it wasn't straight - I was leading the horse. We'd never grown corn before and we'd no idea how to go on with it but you learn quickly. We grew all our own vegetables anyway. I suppose we were better off in some ways, we had butter and milk as well and Mr Abberley used to come with a van from Rudyard with groceries. Before that it was to Hine's Mill for shopping. Nora and Nelly were there in the shop. We had bread from there, 8 loaves a time, walk down the fields and carry it back.

We went to Ramshaw School or Ramshaw College as Alice calls it. We walked from Naychurch of course; there wasn't much traffic on the Buxton Road then. The charabanc buses were running so we sometimes got on that if it was pouring with rain. We had some very good teachers; I was very happy. Mrs Wilde at Rocks Bar sold sweets; she had the big toffee jars. So if it was raining mum gave us money for the bus and living where we did you could see the bus coming and then set off but we were still late for school because we spent the money on sweets and then had to walk anyway.

On Sunday it was to Upperhulme Chapel, morning, noon and night. Ernest Parker was the Sunday school teacher. I thoroughly enjoyed it because it was the only place we went.

We went to Roches Hall to Christmas parties; I shall always remember the mirror in the hall before we went in for tea, it was so massive. I remember the animals there; quite a variety. I used to fill in when the post lady, Mrs Dale from Swainsmoor, had her holidays for 2 or 3 weeks. I used to walk the area from Upperhulme Post Office to the bottom of Goldsitch Moss up past Newstone Chapel to Middle Hills and back. One week to Roches Hall and that way round and another week the other way round. The Yaks seemed terrifying; huge, long haired things but I didn't have any problems. We had to go round the back to the kitchen area with the post and Annie Parker the housekeeper would receive it.

John Pulham, coachman to John Hall, with Katy Hall on Satan, at Ball Haye Hall stable yard.

Then to Well Farm, Stoniers, to Shay (Shaw) Top and Shay Bottom, Harpurs End, Belfields, Jimmy Bloor's tiny house, up to Royal Cottage then all the way back. It was quite a walk; some rough going across the fields and could be very wet and muddy. Mrs Whittaker at Hazel Barrow said I was the best. When it was raining it was miserable but you just kept going. We never had a car so I was used to walking. Swainsmoor was quite a way out and it was dodgy crossing the brook (Churnet).

Pat McCarthy lived at Ferny Knowle down below and I remember when he bought a Tilley lamp. Then he bought one for us. Well, we thought we were in heaven; it was such a wonderful light after oil lamps. The mantles kept breaking, that was a bit of a pest but to us it was a new invention, marvellous.

Later on I lived on Blackshaw Moor alongside the Polish people. The women were so hard working and the men too in the quarries and that and some at Froghall Copper Works and Adams Dairy. I sat with their children and taught them. I lived next door to Victoria; she was in a concentration camp and they'd taken the children and parted them. They were all starving and louse ridden but she survived. Her brother was 14 and all the boys were rounded up and taken off to the gas chambers. She told me some horrific stories. I thought what a difficult and terrible life they'd had.

They used to go hunting in the fields for herbs and things and make an appetising meal out of almost nothing. They were very thrifty, making all the children's clothes, they thought they were well off after what they'd been through.

In 1966 I came to live on Haregate and went to Ball Haye Green Chapel. It was full in those days; like a big family, the happiest days. We had wonderful preachers; old Vernon Egerton, John Sales banging on the pulpit, Cottons from Waterhouses. They came from all over; Bill Sillito invited them. There were jumble sales, coffee mornings, concerts, club day and a choir. It was so sad when all these regulations came in and forced it to close.

Haregate Hall

Christine Kowalski

My grandfather's uncle, Edward Olley was a Colour Sergeant in the army. He came from Essex to Leek in 1872 to give the Queen's Shilling to young men to persuade them to join the army. He decided to settle in Leek, left the army and rented Springhill Farm from the Earl of Macclesfield. The cottage was off Buxton Road and fronted onto the Organ Ground; Springfield Road did not exist in those days.

Springhill Farm. Grandma Adams and Fred under the tree. The building to the left of the house became the first dairy.

Fred Adams II c.1896

He knew nothing about farming so he asked my grandfather Frederick Adams (1st) to come from Little Saling in Essex to Leek to run the farm; he was only 17 years old but had always worked on a farm. In 1885 grandfather bought the stock and farm implements from his uncle for £250 at the rate of £50 a year. He was a hard worker and a good businessman and eventually bought the cottage, the buildings and the land from the Earl of Macclesfield.

Frederick married his cousin, Caroline Byford in 1877. They had six children but five died very young; only my father, Frederick (2nd) survived, born 1894. He worked with my grandfather on the farm until he was in his 20s when he started to work for United Dairies as a salesman. He was given a quota of cheese and butter to sell in a week but as he had the 'gift of the gab' after a few days he had sold his quota and so worked for himself for the rest of the week. He often told me about where he sold his first cheese. He went down to Ecton Cheese Factory where he bought a cheese and then went up to Warslow in his car and sold it to the shop on the corner where there were petrol pumps.

He started to make butter on his father's farm, converting a cowshed into a dairy. He had

Fred Adams II

some big wooden churns and butter packing machines. He bought a van and collected fresh cream every day from Leek Railway Station.

He married my mother, Minnie Hill, in 1914 and she worked hard in the business; she was the niece of Fred Hill who had the book shop on Derby Street. I had two brothers, Frederick (3rd) who was 15 years older than me and John, 6 years older.

In 1925 my father built Springhill House on Buxton Road. We had a young woman to help my mother in the house and a car with a 'dicky' seat. This was the boot of the car which converted into a seat when opened. I loved to sit

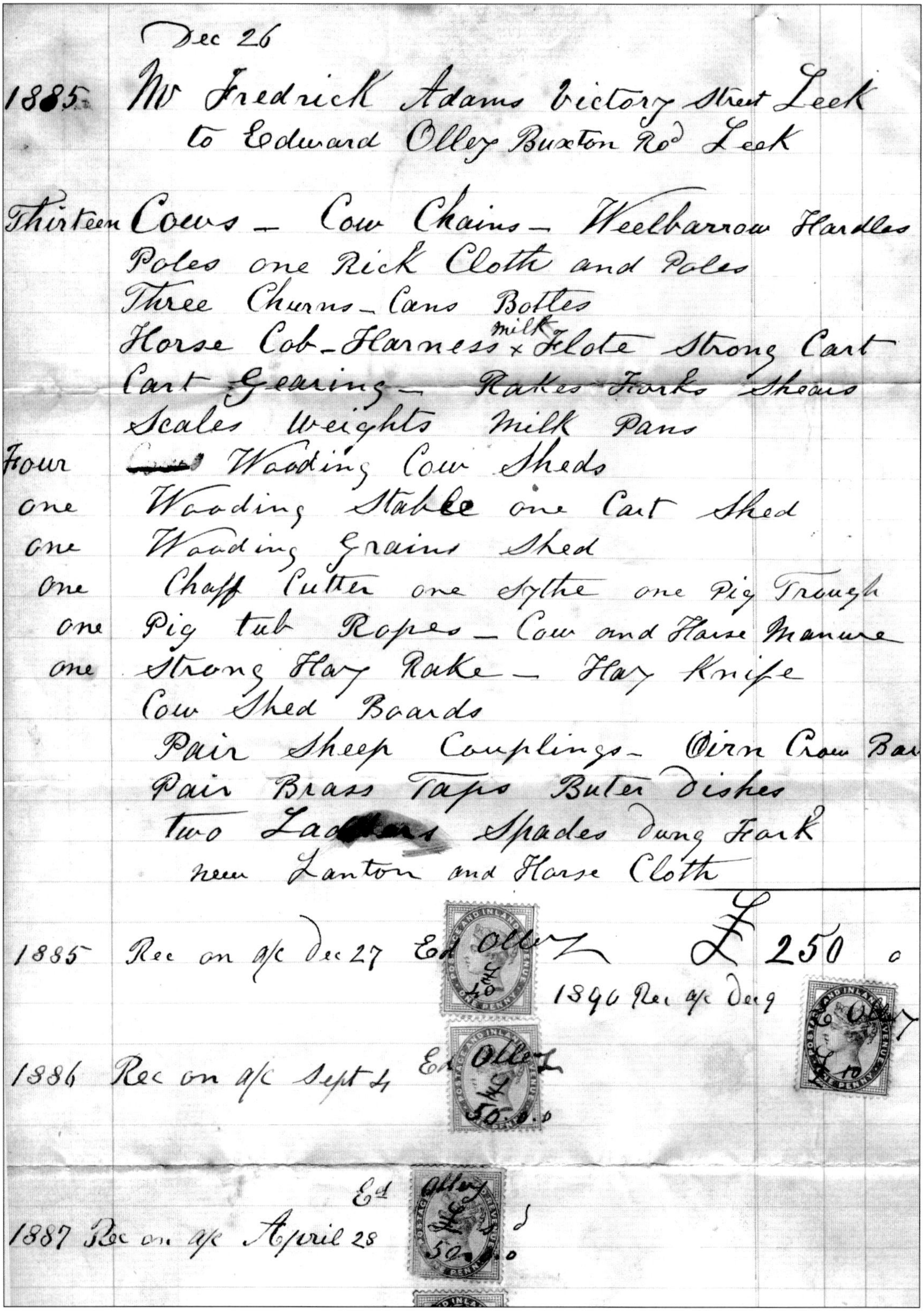

Dec 26

1885 Mr Fredrick Adams Victory Street Leek
   to Edward Olley Buxton Rd Leek

Thirteen Cows — Cow Chains — Weelbarrow Hardles
  Poles one Rick Cloth and Poles
  Three Churns — Cans Botles
  Horse Cob — Harness milk x Flote Strong Cart
  Cart Gearing — Rakes Forks Shears
  Scales Weights Milk Pans
Four Cow Wooding Cow Sheds
one Wooding Stable one Cart Shed
one Wooding Grains Shed
One Chaff Cutter one Sythe one Pig Trough
one Pig tub Ropes — Cow and Horse Manure
one Strong Hay Rake — Hay Knife
  Cow Shed Boards
  Pair Sheep Couplings — Oirn Crow Bar
  Pair Brass Taps Buter dishes
  Two Ladders Spades dung Fork
  new Lanton and Horse Cloth

1885 Rec on a/c dec 27 Ed Olley £ 250 0

         1890 Rec a/c dec 9

1886 Rec on a/c sept 4 Ed Olley

1887 Rec on a/c April 28 Ed Olley

The school in Union St. Fred is at right end in the middle row.

The Bungalow, Buxton Road, was a 1st World War barracks

In Grandad's field near Weston St.
Jean Hill on right, the daughter of Fred Hill

John Kirkland

Grandma's friend, the scandal of Leek
because she wore 'bloomers' to cycle

Springhill House that Fred built but later knocked down to extend the dairy, Christine at the front.

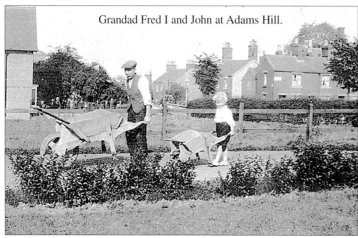

Grandad Fred I and John at Adams Hill.

The Duke of York in Derby Street

in this open seat with our black Labrador dog.

When father was making the butter he'd have a white hat on, then he'd put on his black Homberg hat when he went selling. When my brother Fred was 12 or 13, he used to put on my father's hat and drive the van to the railway station to collect the cream before school.

There were few cars on Buxton Road; we used to sledge and play games on the road. We always had lots of friends and walked or went on our bikes for picnics. The Waste opposite the Moss Rose pub was a favourite playground.

On market day which was Wednesday, drovers would drive sheep and cows down the road and farmers and their families would come into town with horses and traps. I used to love it. One of the drovers was known as Tommy Cold Arse and as he came along we hid behind the gate at Adams and shouted 'Tommy Cold Arse' and then ducked down and he came at us waving his stick. I never knew why they called him that unless it was because he had holes in his trousers. At the time we thought it was hilarious and very daring to shout that to a grown man.

The cattle market was in the centre of the town where Smithfield centre is now. There was the Coffee Tavern and stalls were set out on the corner opposite the monument. The stalls sold fruit, vegetables, meat and household goods and on winter afternoons they were hung with very bright lanterns which made a hissing noise. In Derby Street there was the Duke of York pub where the Leek United is now. There were more stalls there and in the Market Place and of course there was the Butter Market full of all kinds of goods.

Most things were delivered by horse and cart; my grandfather and others such as Bert Hulme delivered milk. Elsie Pember's husband, George delivered coal. Tattons Cafe and Bakers in Derby Street delivered freshly baked bread in a black covered wagon which we children thought looked like something from a cowboy film.

I remember the first council houses on Buxton Road and Shaw Place; Mr Vinen the librarian had one. Eventually more houses were built on Abbotts Road and now of course they stretch all the way to Haregate.

Lower down Buxton Road stood the Pretty Polly stocking factory. They made real silk stockings but unfortunately I was not old enough to wear them. Mr Bull ran the factory and he had a big parrot sitting on a stand in his office. It was a vicious old bird and extremely noisy; we children fed it with nuts - very carefully - it could nip our fingers.

I remember September 3rd 1939; I heard the announcement on the wireless by the Prime Minister, Mr Chamberlain that England had declared war because Germany had invaded Poland. I had no idea what effect the war would have on us. That night the sirens sounded so we thought there was going to be an air raid; father made us put on our gas masks which we had already been given, but nothing happened so we took them off and went to bed.

During the next days and weeks we saw many children coming to Leek to be billeted as evacuees with families. We had no room but many of them came to live nearby. By this time we had moved to a house, still on Buxton Road but opposite Weston Street which we called Adams Hill, Adams after my father's name and Hill because it was mother's maiden name. Food was now rationed and many goods were unobtainable. I don't think people were hungry but we had a very monotonous diet.

Many workers came to Leek from towns like Coventry which had been bombed. They worked in ammunitions factories and other war work. A British restaurant opened at the bottom of Regent Street in a church hall. They sold cheap lunches to workers without a ration book.

Women remodelled their clothes, unravelled hand knitted jumpers and knitted new ones and drew black lines up the back of their legs so it looked as if they were wearing stockings. My mother made some of her clothes to fit me and I wore wooden soled sandals. Occasionally a chemist shop would have some lipsticks in stock; it didn't matter if they were bright orange or purple, the young women bought them and used them and felt fortunate. I was not bothered about such things at the time but before the war ended and for many years afterwards I would have been thrilled to have lovely clothes and cosmetics.

In 1941 my parents were divorced and I went to live in the old farm cottage with my mother. The young woman who had helped mother was called up into the Women's Army where she became a sergeant. My brother John joined the army and served in Europe and Egypt. Fred volunteered for the air force but was turned down because of poor eyesight. He was now running

Adams Dairies, had married and I had a nephew, Frederick (4th).

I became very upset with all the changes in my life; I became disobedient and didn't bother with school work or home work. In those days, unlike today, women had a very poor deal after a divorce. My father had to pay my mother an allowance which would stop if she remarried and he paid an allowance for me which would stop when I was 18. So mother spent all my allowance sending me away to boarding school, Penrhos College. I said I would run away but of course I didn't. It was the best thing she could have done for me actually; a complete new start.

As it was wartime the Ministry of Food took over our school in Colwyn Bay because it was the safest place to be in Wales. Chatsworth House in Derbyshire was offered to us or to soldiers as a billet. The Duke of Devonshire decided that a girl's school would make better tenants than soldiers and so I lived at Chatsworth from 1942 until June 1945. I made many friends; my best friend still writes to me to this day. But most importantly at that time there were other girls there with divorced parents so I did not feel the odd one out.

I slept in the State bedroom; there were 16 of us and we changed rooms each year. It was very grand and so beautiful with embossed leather and ceilings painted with naked figures.

We got up at 7.30; there were 250 girls and obviously not enough bathrooms so they built long rows of wash bowls where we washed all over with a flannel. It could be very cold but there was no escape and there was a rota of two baths a week for each girl which was strictly enforced.

After washing we made our beds which consisted of straw pallets, tidied our drawers and went down to breakfast in what had been the servant's dining room; they were very big because so many people had been employed at Chatsworth. Breakfast was not very exciting with it being wartime; just sliced bread and a piece of margarine as big as a penny and then sometimes a hard boiled egg. What old bread they had was put into the oven and baked hard and brown like a rusk and we had that with a drink at break time at 10 o'clock. We were hungry and ate what was put in front of us and I have never been faddy about food ever since.

We had lessons in beautiful rooms; one had been where Mary Queen of Scots had been a prisoner of Elizabeth I. In the afternoons we played hockey and lacrosse or cricket and tennis in summer. If the weather was wet we put on our wellingtons and macs and walked through the woods to the hunting tower where there was a prefect to do a roll call to check that you'd done the walk. At the top are two pools which feed the fountains and in summer we were allowed to swim in them. In winter we skated on the Long Water Lake; sometimes called the Canal pond where the Emperor Fountain was in the garden.

After 'prep' and our evening meal we went to our dormitories. The young ones had lights out at 8.30 and the older ones 9 o'clock. We used to do each other's hair though we weren't supposed to and I remember once, one girl's mother had sent her some oranges - can you imagine in wartime? She brought them into the bedroom, which wasn't allowed, food in the bedroom. We were peeling these oranges when the French teacher came round and she said, 'What on earth do you think you gals are doing, get up at once, dress yourselves and take those rollers out of your hair!' So we had to completely dress ourselves in uniform, long stockings and all and stand in the corridor where she gave us each a newspaper and we had to learn a paragraph by heart which we had to repeat to her to prove we'd learnt it then we were allowed back to bed. This was 2 o'clock in the morning and I had a French exam the next day which she was not pleased about.

There was a very sad time when the Duke's son, the Marquis of Hartington was killed during the war. His uniform and swords arrived back home at Chatsworth in a big basket. We were all upset; they were such a nice family.

Early packing machines

Lomas's shop, corner of Southbank St c. 1960.

I was sorry when it was time to leave; I had worked hard and done well there. It was quite a shock going back to the little cottage after the big rooms at Chatsworth. I went to work in the laboratory at Adams. We now imported butter from Australia, New Zealand, Denmark and Holland. England was not able to produce enough milk and butter was still rationed. The butter was blended and packed. I tested butter for salt, moisture and keeping qualities; we made a special butter with a high percentage of salt for Welsh miners which they liked.

We went to dances at the Town Hall; there wasn't much in the way of refreshments - a cup of tea and a biscuit or paste sandwiches perhaps. I met a Polish soldier who had come to England after fighting in Italy. He had been a prisoner of war and couldn't go back to Poland because it was occupied by Russian Communists. He clicked his heels, bowed and said, 'Would you like to dance?' that's all he could say in English, he was very dashing.

He was demobbed and sent to work in the steel factories in Wolverhampton; Polish personnel could only work in steel, coal or stone so some went to the quarries around Buxton. George went to work in the steel industry and others went to the coal mines around Stoke. Then after a time they were allowed to find other work and my brother said, 'If you like, come and work at the dairy.' So he became a joiner there; he loved working with wood and went to Stoke College to learn the trade.

Fred II in 1947 on Blackshaw Moor.

Christine with skates and Jaguar SS in the Park.

We married in 1948 and went to night school at Leek College; they started classes for wives of Poles, you could learn Polish and the Poles learned English. I took some years out of work in the 1950s when I had our children then went back until my mother had a stroke. Adams had gone from strength to strength; the lorries were 'spreading everywhere'. The workforce had increased to 3,000 including the printing works in Queen Street, Elkes biscuits and a factory near Waltham Abbey. We had our own repair shops, our own painters, joiners and plumbers. It used to tickle me when I went to boarding school; I never thought about being part of Adams. It was written on my trunk and they asked, 'Are you Adams from Leek, does your father have a butter factory?' It was no big deal for me then.

Eventually the business was taken over by the Irish Dairy Board, they told my brother that they would keep the name Adams and he was very disappointed when it was changed to Kerrygold. I thought it was a shame that he didn't live to see the name changed back to Adams Foods in 2010.

On Cat Tor.

CATTLE MARKET, L...

GERMAN GIPSIES
AT LEEK HORSE FAIR
OCT. 17, '06.

**OLD LEEK
MARKET**

Leek Market c.1960

The District Officer, Bill Ratcliffe 3rd from left, at Leek Market c.1950.

The District Officer for Staffs Agricultural Executive Committee (commonly known as War Ag) which later became the NAAS (National Agricultural Advisory Service).

Bill Badham

1st September 1939 I was 10 years old. We all turned up for school, those of us that were going to be evacuated, with our cases, gas mask and a ticket round our neck with our name and address on. That was Columbia Road School, Bethnal Green and we walked from there about a mile to Cambridge Heath station where we got on a train and got out a few hours later at North Walsham in Norfolk.

We were assigned to various houses and I went to a local milkman's house. I was there for 10 days and then selected with 15 other lads to live at a gentleman's residence called Hoveton Hall just outside Wroxham. We went there and we had a butler, a footman, a housekeeper, and two ladies besides, to look after us. We were taught etiquette, how to address people especially the landed gentry who would come and look at these little so and so's from the East End of London.

Everyone who came always brought us a present of some description and the night before they came we all drew for short straws as to who would make the speech of thank you and in this particular case a Mr Storey, who had a very large estate, came and he fetched a box of oranges for us and I'd drawn the short straw the night before so it was my job to stand up and make a speech thanking him. I was shaking like a leaf.

Our parents weren't happy about us being evacuated but we thought it was a great adventure, which it was for the first week. Everything was totally strange; we were waited on hand and foot it was out of this world. Afterwards it started wearing off. My family were a working family, two very good parents and two sisters. We had a good school and a good education; some in my class were out of poverty - we had some very poor and some very rich. Our parents came to see us about once a month. They always came down on the train, had their lunch in Wroxham and then walked the mile and a bit to the hall. We were always pleased to see them. We used to write to each other of course.

We had a very good life there; as somebody once said, we lived like Little Lord Fauntleroy. Of course Dunkirk came along and we were playing cricket in the field when we heard some aeroplanes coming very low and the master in charge shouted 'Hit the deck!' which we did. Just at that time we heard machine gun bullets flying and it was two Spitfires chasing another plane which turned out, we found out the day after, to be a friendly Pole that had escaped from France and was just coming over. It was fortunate that our chaps missed it and he landed safely.

We stayed there till 1st June 1940. The night before the headmaster came to us and said 'We're going to South Wales.' So we got the map out to look at this place in South Wales because we couldn't pronounce it. The following morning we gathered our belongings up and we all marched down to Wroxham station and got on the train for South Wales. Eventually, after many hours travelling we got out at LEEK station where we were put on various buses. I got on one and we went to Rushton School where Mrs Robinson picked two of us out; the other was Pat Steadman. We went to live with them at High Lea in Rushton James and afterwards when they moved to Pheasants Clough in 1942.

When Pat was 14 he left school and went back to his parents - he said he never wanted to see another green field again. I took to it like a duck to water. I liked the cattle, learned how to milk by hand and even entered the Young Farmers milking competitions later on. I enjoyed it at Pheasants Clough, I've got a soft spot for it to this day, High Lea also.

I went back to London and did two years in a solicitor's office. I was back there for the Doodlebugs and the rockets. Doodlebugs weren't so bad; they were like an old Fordson tractor, you could hear them coming, look up and see them. If they stopped you hit the deck. One night three of us were walking from being at the ATC and we heard this one coming. We looked up and I could have thrown a stone at it; it was just above us. It looked as though it would hit the chimneys across at the undertakers. We hit the deck - it stopped as it went past going down quarter of a mile further on where it blew up and killed 146 that night.

That you thought was bad but rockets were more frightening because you didn't hear them; you saw a blue flash in the sky, you dropped and you were just lucky (or unlucky) where it came down. When I first went back in 1944, Doodlebugs were going over and it was frightening but you adopted an attitude, 'Well, if it's my turn....' so you went about your normal business because they came over day and night, 24 hours a day. Of course there were some that couldn't cope with it.

In my job, the young men had gone to war, left in the office were old men and young girls so I had to do all the outside work. I got round London like Billy-ho. I was busy and all expenses paid but I was doing the job and studying law at the same time and I got close to a breakdown. So when I saw the doctor, he was one of the old school and he said 'You're doing too much; you should get out of this job.' I said 'What about going back farming?' he said 'You couldn't do better, get out in the open air.' So that was it; I came back to Pheasants Clough and stopped there till I married Marjorie and we went farming on our own account.

Marjorie Badham

We moved to the Homestead, Upperhulme from Worcestershire in 1942. My dad had a young man and an old man who worked for him and the young man would have been exempt from joining up as he was a farmworker but his mates had gone in the army and he thought he was missing out so he volunteered. That left one old man, they were on a tenanted farm and the landlord wouldn't do any repairs and he went off abroad for the winter. The estate was going to pot so we ended up coming to Staffordshire.

Mum had people to live in till the single bed sheets were well worn; I was in a single bed where the sheets were getting extinct; they'd been patched till you couldn't go any more. So she went to see whether she could get any extra coupons towards bedding and they said 'Were you newly married or bombed out?' she replied 'Well, neither.' So they said 'Hard Luck; you can't have any.'

In the winter of 1947 the snowdrifts were 8-10 foot deep between the Homestead and the Paddock but we could go on sledges downhill from the gate into Moses Lane and land right past the boiler hole to the canteen at Tattons. Then old David Mycock from Naychurch, the roadman he complained about us sledging and come and put some ashes down from the boiler hole. There was no traffic - it couldna get.

Band of Hope 1907

Proclamation of King George V 1910.

Outside Greystones mid 1930s.

Tattons c.1950s Derby Street

Club Day probably 1940s

C.1908, end of Derby Street looking at 'Sparrow Park'

C.1913, end of Derby Street

Lilian Webb

Our family, the Millans lived in Bethnal Green. My dad was a journeyman, he used to make suitcases and my mum used to line 'em. On September 1st 1939 me and my two brothers, Ken and Stan were in the hall of Columbia Road School with our parents. I was 10, Ken 8 and Stan was 6 the day war broke out, September 3rd.

Marjorie & Alf on Fanny at Brownslow with George.

We thought we were all going on holiday and we'd be back again in a couple of weeks; that's what the teachers had told us. We made our way to the station in the East End of London with a gas mask over our shoulders, a bag of goodies and a big label with our name on pinned on our coats. I couldn't make out why all the mothers were in tears.

When we got to the platform there were soldiers and sailors who threw pennies to us and wished us luck. We got told off for pickin' 'em up - I suppose in case we fell on the lines, you know what kids are; runnin' about.

The train blew its whistle, steam and smoke shot out and with a screeching noise we were off, waving to our mums and dads. The train took us to Norfolk and we landed up in Wroxham, a very pretty place and there we were herded into this big hall. Ladies came and picked out the children they'd like to take care of. 'I'll have this one' and 'I'll have that one.' We were the last 3 because my mum had said, 'Look after the two boys.' And so I stood there hanging on to my brothers' hands and wouldn't let them go and saying, 'My mum says we gotta stay together.' And people only wanted 1 or 2. So this Mrs Harmer, she said, 'Well, I'll take them.' And she'd already got two boys of her own. Her and her husband were very good to us; they had a lovely bungalow by the dykes. We had never been to the

Lily, Tom Beswick, Mrs Millan and Ken & Stan.

country or the sea before; we'd never been well enough off. We thought it was great.

We stayed for about a year and then the bombing started down there so they decided to move us to a safer place, the Midlands. The sad part was my brothers were sent to Bradnop, I didn't know where and I cried my eyes out. A few of us girls landed up in Horton. Ivy went to stay with the post mistress in Rudyard, Doris on Bill Needham's farm and a lady called Mrs Beswick took

C.1930

C.1960

DERBY STREET, LEEK.

me into Brownslow Farm where her husband, George was and his sister, Mabel and the old granddad, as I called George's father. They all stared at me as I walked in; the old granddad said, 'She is the funniest boy I've seen, she's all arms and legs.' I was a skinny, white-faced Londoner.

I settled in; I had a room of my own which I never had before and a little lamp to take up to bed, there was no electricity then. Back in London we had a gas mantle that used to hiss when you lit it. I couldn't make out why there were no shops for miles, I couldn't run to the shop and buy a penny Golly bar or a ha'penny worth of sweets like I did in Wroxham or London. If I wanted any I'd have to walk to Rudyard, which seemed the end of the world to me.

I thought the countryside was lovely but it was all so strange; I'd never seen cows, sheep, pigs or horses so near, it frightened me a bit I can tell you. Dora found out where my brothers were and took me to see them at Railway Cottages, Bradnop the home of Mr and Mrs Bunce. They had no children of their own so really made a fuss of Ken and Stan - we were all happy!

A little while after I was there, Dora had a little boy, Philip; I thought the world of him. One day when George and Dora went to Leek Market I was left to look after little Philip when the old granddad came in and said, 'I need your help, a cow is calving and its foot is caught.' I put Philip in the pram and went over to the shippon. He had some rope which he put round the calf somehow and he told me to pull the rope gently while he saw to the cow. We eventually pulled the calf out but the funny thing was I took it all in my stride for a townie.

I learned to milk cows by hand and one day George put me where a pig was farrowing. He said, 'You sit on that stool.' Because they were busy milking. 'And if that ones dead, put it in the slopstone and put the others near the pig but mind the pig doesn't get up and lay on 'em.' I was sitting there when my mum come to see us and she went mad; she couldn't think I could do anything like that, I was a town girl not a country girl.

There was no school for us; it was all full up so we was in the cricket field in the pavilion and we used to learn nature studies and ballroom dancing until they could fit us in Leek school.

Monday was washday. We had a big dolly tub and a posser. Put the washing in the tub and twist it round with the posser then put it in the boiler, rinse and hang it on the line. There was no bathroom either; I had a big tin bath in the dairy house - it was none too warm in the winter!

Mum and dad moved to Stafford to be nearer to us as she had been fretting for us. Some people took parents in and Mr and Mrs Kenny took ours in. They came to the farm bringing my brothers; it was lovely to see them. Ken and Stan even came for a holiday. George took Stan with him shooting game one day with the dog. He said to the dog 'Clap.' And the dog lay down very quiet but dear Stan jumped up and clapped his hands. All Hell let loose, the birds flew away, George went mad and the poor dog didn't know what to do. That's townies for you!

We all went to see Dora's mum and dad in Wincle. I went out to play with Nelly and Jimmy throwing sticky bobs. I ran across the concrete as I thought and just sank in - it was a midden. They ran for George who put a big plank of wood across and threw me a rope. He lay across the plank and pulled me in. Did I stink? They put the hose pipe on me and all thought it was very funny. I came home in some of Nelly's clothes. What a day!

I stayed on the farm until my mother was taken ill; I was 14. She had a tumour on the brain and was sent to Christies where she later died so I had to go to Stafford and look after my brothers who were still at school and living with dad. I worked making leather leggings or gaiters and saved up for a suit for my brother to go to work in when he left school.

After a while dad found a place for us and we moved back to London but over the years I've always kept in touch with the Beswick family and visited regularly.

Henry Davenport,
Grandma Hulme's
brother from the Black
Swan, in light suit.

Great-grandparents,
Mr & Mrs Peter
Walwyn, Novi Lane.

Great-grandfather Francis
Wint in 1906 aged 87.
He had a small farm in
Broad Street.

Uncle Will Walwyn,
Grandma Wint's brother.
The horse was called Dolly

Kath Wint, Mary Nixon

Our granddad, Samuel Platt Hulme was born in 1857 at an inn and small farm at Bridge End, Leek. There were 21 children - grandma said there were 21 twice because one died and then great grandma had another. He passed a labour exam when he was 12 and started work apprenticed to a joiner. He became a journeyman joiner working for Graces' builders of Cruso Street.

He took up with grandma, she was a Davenport from the Black Swan and a lot younger than him and they eloped. They lived at Watercroft at Abbey Green by the Churnet. There was a big garden and they grew a lot of vegetables and kept pigs and a stirk or two. When granddad killed a pig he hung it in the cherry tree to cool; there was nowhere else. Mother used to fetch his wages and she used to say they would see Colonel Nicholson's coach drive past driven by Victor Steele and how smart he was.

Uncle Enoch fell in the Churnet when he was two and a half and grandma jumped straight in after him even though she couldn't swim. Fortunately there was a man who could swim looking over the bridge and he got them out. It could have been tragic.

Our dad, John Wint joined up aged 18 in 1917. He was with the West Yorkshire Regiment and was what was called a runner. He was with another private soldier and an officer and they went looking round to see where they could take the main troop of men in the night to dig in. The chef at the Officer's mess came from the same town as the other young soldier and they were always hungry so they used to sleep on the steps and the cook would come out and give them a half bowl of custard or something and half a loaf. These cooks were better than some he told us; they could make bully beef taste lovely.

Eventually in Belgium, a shell came over the top and dad was wounded. There were a lot of stretcher cases so he said he'd walk down to the field hospital which he did and then fainted; perhaps from loss of blood. When he came round there were two men looking down at him and one said 'Oh it will have to come off poor kid.' The other said, 'Well I don't know.' So they didn't take his arm off but he was in hospital a good while. We have the letters that the sister sent to grandma about it. He was sent back to Bradford in the winter. He said it was the coldest winter he'd ever experienced but the people had the warmest hearts.

In the 1920s he worked in a silk mill as an overseer. Granddad Wint had a field or two and kept hens in one at Thorncliffe on the side of Morridge so dad had an idea of farming so he rented Manor Farm from Mr Salt at Derby in 1930. At one time it was in Bradnop Manor and known as Lower Acre and the other farm Upper Acre.

We'd go to Leek on Wednesdays with the horse and trap, 'parking it up' at the Black Swan. It was quite an event for young children. Mother occasionally sold butter in the Butter Market. We had a black box which fitted in the trap and grandma used to get bread from Tattons for us and we'd fill the box up. You left a list in the shops and groceries would be put up ready for you to pick up. 'When would you like it for?' they asked. We went to Jack Balls in Sheepmarket for years, later to Pickfords. Then you went to the butchers and got your meat.

Grandma Wint lived on Abbotts Road and we went and had dinner there; the horse stood outside. Uncle Will - William Walwyn used to come for his dinner too because his wife had died young. We remember he ate rice pudding with a knife. He'd been with horses in the army in the First War. He had a few cows on Novi Lane; there were fields there then. He milked them and sold his own milk, measured out of the churn on a round.

On the way back we had to get out of the trap and walk up Easing Lane to ease the horse's

The Hollies, on corner of Novi Lane and Abbotts Rd, built by Peter Walwyn 1887

Uncle Enoch Hulme, Aunt Harriet, William, Harry, Ernest and Annie. In his youth Uncle Enoch travelled with Wombwells Circus, we think working with the elephants.

BELOW:
St. Luke's School
John Wint is 3rd from
left, 2nd row down.

burden. It was very steep and rough and our lane was very rough too. When dad got to our land he used to take the horse off the road and onto the field and stand up in the trap with the reins so he could pick the horses head up if it stumbled. Then he could let it go faster.

When it was icy he had a little cloth bag with studs in and his hammer and when we got to the shed on Easing Lane he'd knock the flats out and put the sharps in the shoes. Phyllis was an eager horse; dad liked her and we also had Fanny, she was black. At one time we had an old war horse; it went with a bit of sideways gait and quite fast.

There were bad snows in the war years. We filled everything we'd got up with milk - baths, old churns and we even fed some back to the cows because we hadn't much corn - Dad carried it on his back up from Buxtons. We couldn't even take the horse; we hadn't got a road out. Dad also dug the churns out of the snow, the empties, and carried them back too. There was too much snow even for us to use a sledge in 1947. It was all built up with snow in the bottom over the brook and things

The Moss Rose 1947

travelled over it. Every time we did dig the road clear it snowed and blowed and filled it in again.

Letters from France

21-9-17

Dear Mrs Wint,

Your son Pte Wint has been admitted to this hospital seriously wounded in the arm. You probably will be contacted by the War Office that he is 'dangerously ill' His condition is serious. Every thing that possibly can be done for him will be done.

I will write you again in a day or two

Yours sincerely B. Alder (Sister)

No 3. C.C.B. France   22-9-17

Dear Mrs Wint,

I am pleased to write and inform you your little boy is much better than when I wrote you yesterday. He is very bright, an excellent patient and I trust will make a good recovery. He will write you himself in a day or two but I want him to rest as much as possible.

23-9-17

Dear Mrs Wint,

Your little boy I'm pleased to say is much better than when I wrote you a few days ago. We hope now to be able to save his arm. His wound is still serious but hope with every possible care he will make a good recovery.

30-9-17

I received your wire of yesterday and am very pleased to be able to report a considerable improvement in your 'laddie's' arm. His arm and elbow joint was very badly smashed up and the surgeons feared the arm would have to be amputated but at present it is making very good progress.

John is quite happy in the ward with several other boys about his own age and he is a good patient. He sends best love to you all and says you are not to worry about him. I will write you again soon.

I am yours sincerely, B. Alder (Sister)

11-10-17

Dear Miss Walwyn,

Thank you very much for your kind letter. I make a point of writing or see that the mothers, wives or nearest relatives of my patients are written to. I know in some cases how very anxious the home people are.

Your nephew John is making good steady progress. I have been away from my ward for a few days opening up a new eye ward but returned yesterday and can see a great improvement. Capt King the Medical Officer has taken a great interest in his wound. The elbow joint has been excised which will result in loss of some movement but in time it will be quite a useful arm. For three days it was feared amputation would be necessary but am glad to say that danger has passed.

Just now John is sound asleep. He really is a plucky little chap. He assures me he is not little. Will you kindly let his mother know he is improving. I will write her tomorrow.

Yours very sincerely,

Betty Alder

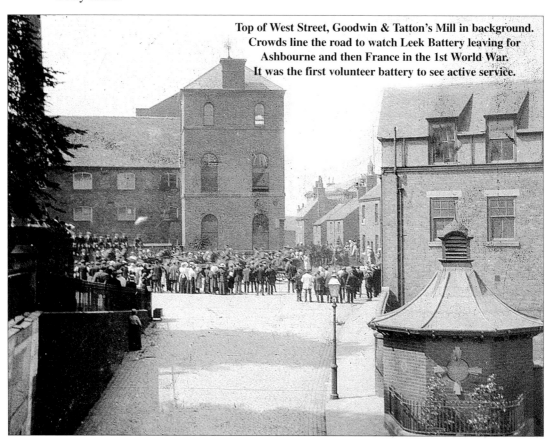

Top of West Street, Goodwin & Tatton's Mill in background. Crowds line the road to watch Leek Battery leaving for Ashbourne and then France in the 1st World War. It was the first volunteer battery to see active service.

James Street c.1915

Buxton Road c.1915

Stanley Street above and Derby Street below, c.1920

A Moorland Childhood

I was born at Morridge Top Farm in 1926 - up to now perhaps the last one to be born there. I went to Flash School for 8 and a half years and then I had 3 months at Leek before leaving at Christmas aged 14. Walking to school, over a mile and a half, the roads were quieter but it must have been one of the bleakest roads anyone could have walked in wintertime. Sometimes if it was windy you had to turn your back and walk into it like that. I remember having a little fur muff and that was wonderful and a scarf and it was all tied down around your waist. But we had good attendance. You couldn't stay away because the inspector would be after you.

When I was 6 and my brother 12, it started snowing one Friday and it snowed for 3 days non stop. My father was posting and he had the presence of mind on the Friday when it started, to get us out of school when he delivered the post otherwise we would never have got. We walked down the churchyard and straight down onto the road. It was freezing to that extent, there were steam lorries abandoned all the way up the road, you could walk off their roofs anywhere into the fields; a very hard time that was, 1932/33.

Dad's name was Vauncey and he was postman at Flash. He started off at Flash Post Office, went down the Back o'th'Cross, over to Cut Thorn Hill and Three Shires, back into Knotbury and near to where the mushroom farm was started, Turncliffe Farm. All round the outskirts -16 miles. He used to come back by Brandside and out at the shop, the Woodstores, then back to the Post Office. It was 6 days a week with one week's holiday which he'd try and get round haytime then mother would do the posting because we needed the money.

You couldn't do the round as you thought. Someone had done it and you had got to do it in that time. But there were little small holdings and some of the farmers went into the quarries to work and their wives had to look after things - something would happen to a cow or calf and father would help them out.

I had to put Dubbin on his boots every night. They didn't have the lightweight uniforms like they have today. He had to wear full uniform for the winter which was flat cap and a big heavy coat which I would imagine when it was wet through and the big heavy boots and his bag could weigh a hundredweight.

He had Boxing Day off but not Christmas Day. We never had Christmas Day as a family; he did 2 rounds. He had to be at the Post Office for 6 o'clock so needed to get up at half past 4 because he always had a fry, bacon, whatever before he went out. They posted all sorts of things in those days, even beef from London and he had to carry that round. He had to come back at least once and be loaded again because there was so much mail and Christmas Day there was more than any other day and so we never saw him until about 11 o'clock at night.

He was a stretcher bearer in the First War but I never knew; he never talked about it.

There was a farm at Harpur Hill where the college was, called Burlow Grange which was where father was born. Then granddad moved to Pyeclough and then Oakenclough. Beresfords lived at Hocker, next to it and Phyllis once told me that they used to get a saddle and go and catch Mr Philip's (granddad) horse and ride it round after 10 o'clock at night. What they used to get up to! Another thing was whitewashing horses' tails.

The Bradburys kept the smithy at Shining Ford and we used to have the horse shod there. We took it down to Oakenclough and waited there while they took it down with their horse. We only had a halter on it; it was very quiet. While they were gone I would do little jobs like feeding cade lambs.

When father came out of the army granddad rented Morridge Top for him from the Harpur-Crewe estate. It was 65 acres and he kept 4 to 6 milking cows and some young stock. Sometimes he'd have an in-calf heifer and walk it to the auction at Flash. It was in its hey-day when I was at school; at play time you could go out and see.

When we milked, we didn't have the water to cool the milk so mother made butter. She had a very good round in Leek, going as far as Westwood. If we'd worked hard in the hay field I had a treat and went with mother in the summer holidays on the bus. When she first started she used to go with Mrs Mellor from next door in the horse and trap. She wouldn't have as much then; there weren't as many cows.

She kept the butter on a bench on the pantry floor which was like being in a fridge because the pantry was at the back of the house where the sun sets. She wrapped it in dock leaves which we gathered at the roadside and then put it in a basket covered with a white cloth to take to Leek.

She used to go to the lady who did the dinners for the market where the farmers went for their meat and potato pie and egg custard. She had a good round for eggs too. A lot of people used to walk from Meerbrook with their butter baskets carrying 10 or 12 pounds of butter and

Auctioneers Announcements

MESSRS. S. MOTTRAM & SONS

LEEK CATTLE MARKET
On Wednesday next at 11 o'clock
100 DAIRY COWS AND HEIFERS.
150 BARREN CATTLE.
50 CALVES AND SHEEP.
Poultry and Sundries.

WARSLOW STOCK SALE
Friday, June 19, at 12.30
100 DAIRY AND STORE CATTLE.
Sundries including Fencing Stakes, Gates, etc.

FLASH CATTLE MARKET
Friday, June 26

Leek Market Place c.1920s

eggs too. It would weigh heavy before you'd walked all the way.

Then a lot of people used to stand the market and if your eggs were browner and bigger you'd sell them quicker than anyone else and even if the white ones were as big they didn't go as well. It must have been very hard to carry their eggs and butter in and then stand waiting for people to come or they'd walk past and have a look and some would get their thumb nail and scrape a bit off if they weren't quite sure.

It was easier for mother, she could go in at 9 o'clock, get round as quick as she could and get the bus back. There was a very good grocer, Balls in Sheepmarket and she could leave her baskets there -- she got her groceries there - and have a look up the stalls; they sold everything then.

The Club Feast at Flash was a good day out for country people. It was amazing; there must have been hundreds there; they say charabancs came even from Sheffield. Some would come on the first bus and stay in the New Inn until the last bus so you can imagine what that was like. We had donkey rides and we were athletic; I loved events like Jubilees because I did very well in the races and competitions.

I used to look forward to haytime; we mowed 16 acres. We had the little buildings where we kept the young stock away from the house and it wasn't worth going back for meals so mother used to make a picnic. I thought that was grand having a picnic in the hayfield but mother didn't because of the insects.

There were lots of curlews and the moors were covered in grouse. There were more birds then because there was a gamekeeper, Mr Beswick from Flash Bar. On the moors around Morridge Top were beaters when they were shooting and occasionally you found a grouse that hadn't been picked up. That was a treat but not for me because they tasted of the heather.

The war was on, the bombers going over and sirens going. A bomber crashed at the back of the Roches; I remember going to school and the boys from Moss End told us what had happened. So when we got back home Mother said, 'We'll go down and see what's happened.' Because it was such a crash; it shook the place, you didn't know what had gone off in the night, the bed shook.

We couldn't believe it; it was all burnt out in the bottom and the Home Guard were standing round, but the bodies of the German airmen had never been moved so as we stood on the top of the hill, you could have just walked down and touched them. We didn't have time to think much about it because we had to get back again.

In those last 3 months at school in Leek we were in the air raid shelters a lot. You could be doing gym and the sirens would go, the teachers would say 'Don't panic girls, don't panic.' We didn't have time to get properly dressed and had to walk very orderly down to the shelters.

I had a bicycle when the buses didn't run; the Americans were on the road then and the lorries would come past and they'd whistle at you and nearly take you with them; you had to stick on to your bike. I worked for a while in a grocery shop then went to work on a farm at Bradnop doing farm and dairy work. I lived in and went home most Sundays on my bicycle to Morridge Top. You could free-wheel down but you'd got to get up first which meant a lot of pushing and standing up on the pedals.

They were coming out of chapel at Upperhulme one Sunday night as I was going past. Someone told my mother on the bus the following Wednesday. She said, 'If I hear that again, you won't have a bike!' I must have been going too fast; I didn't even see the people standing there. It was good - all downhill by Rocks Bar and Winking Man.

D P.

St. Edward Street c.1920. Right, at bottom, a Sigley's coach coming from the Station.

Snow Plough c.1920

Newcastle Road above the Station Bridge c.1910

c.1930

Colin Shenton

My father, James Shenton from Leek, went to Canada for 3 years when he was young but when the First World War broke out he came back, joined up and went in the trenches in France. He came out of the army in 1918 and I think received £100 for fighting. So with that he started up knackering at Goats Fell, Bottomhouse in partnership with Edgar Simcock from the Travellers Rest at Bottomhouse.

James and Stella Shenton early 1950s

He was there until 1922 when he moved to Easing Moor Farm, Thorncliffe. There was then a thatched cottage facing south. Gordon Barlow worked for my father for about 40 years and he moved into the cottage. There was also a stable and dad had two wooden bungalows erected at the bottom of the drive - I think they had been an Officers' Mess in the war - and he moved in there. Gordon used to get a lot of drink and came in one night blind drunk. The fire had just gone out so he threw paraffin on and struck a match and burnt the roof off the cottage. Dad had it rebuilt in 1926.

At that time Thorncliffe had no electric, no mains water or sewerage. The only water supply for us was through land drains and it ran dry in summertime so we had to fetch water from the village brook in 40 gallon drums.

In the first instance dad would be supplying one or two zoos and he used to send meat by rail down to London. Of course if it went wrong on the way you didn't get paid; there were no fridges. He used to fetch ice from Bosley Ice Factory; I once went with him to fetch bags of ice.

In the early days he had a horse and a cart with a hand winch and a ramp on the back but then had one of the first Model T Ford wagons that came into Leek. When I was a child I remember he had a Morris Commercial truck which braked only on the rear and a Bedford as well which he used to run alternately. He was a licensed horse slaughterer - they had to be licensed for horses then but not cattle, that came later. It was on the door of the wagon-James Shenton Licensed Horse Slaughterer.

The meat was never for human consumption; in the second war he leased a shop in Pall Mall, Hanley selling dog and cat meat. There were huge signs in the shop - This Meat Is Unfit for Human Consumption and it had to be dyed with a green vegetable dye so if people bought it, it was obvious. Loads of people queued up there. It was sold by the pound, completely boned out. In the slaughterhouse. There was a big iron pole running across from side to side and they strung up a fore and hind leg over it, opened the animal up, skinned it round and stripped the hide down one side and then changed over and did the other side. Then they took each quarter off and boned it out. The meat was then taken to Hanley and dyed as it was sold. I suppose if someone wanted to trim the dyed meat off and eat it, they could but the dye was very searching and they'd have been hard up to do it but then during the war some people may have been desperate.

There were two auctioneers in Leek market until 1960 when they closed Heywood Street.

Joe Gilman with his Auntie,
Mary Brown at Ankers
Lane Farm, Thorncliffe.

Mrs Piercy,
c.1930 in
Ankers Lane.

Colin Shenton
with Alec
Brown's cart
and Smoky, and
possibly Alec
on the load,
1946

They each had a ring, Mottrams and Ashes. Dad would go in on a Wednesday and buy several cattle; they might have Johnes Disease or be coughing with TB. Some poor cattle he turned out on Morridge to try, some went on all right, they'd just been short of food, clemmed. He bought forty acres of land, Pillwill, off Easing Lane with a barn. He dealt in various things; pigs, cattle, motor cars - it was just after the war when you couldn't get new cars.

When I was 11, I started having a day off on a Wednesday and going into the market with my dad. He would always go into Mottrams where there were more thin cattle; there was a better quality cow in Ashes and so I went into Ashes and he'd given me a good idea even then of what meat a beast would cut and how much it was worth to buy. I used to go up to £6 or £7 for a thin cow then. I would be bidding against Don Weston from Lordshire Farm and other Westons. I was a little lad of 11 with a cap on, having to get on the top rail to get noticed and the dealers didn't like me being there. It went on for a few weeks until one of the lads at school shopped me; I shouldn't have been doing it anyway.

So most of the animals were screw cows; the dead ones might have had iyant (blackleg) which caused sudden death mainly in young cattle or bloat where clover had caused them to blow up with gas and even burst their stomachs. From the Market Drayton area, grass staggers was a problem. There came some big cattle from George Porter; he was a local preacher from that area who got around the markets and had a cattle wagon in the early 50s. It was always busy though it quietened off during the summer. There were a few other suppliers like Tom Brassington before he had his own yard, he'd roll up at 7 o'clock at night with one or two on his wagon.

All of my life we had a phone but before that it was all by letter. In my time we had quite a few cattle in under the 'order' for TB. The government paid the farmer so much and we paid so much, that was before regular TB testing came in. And there were one or two cases of Anthrax; Aubrey Boden who worked for my father actually contracted it but was one of the lucky ones to get over it. I remember questioning it on a farm once; if the animal had been dead for a while and the nose was still bleeding, there was something wrong and it was suspected anthrax. I said to the farmer, 'Have you had this cleared with the vet?' 'Oh yes, he's been out.' So I paid for the cow - £5 then. When I got back to the yard, Gordon Barlow - who'd had plenty of experience - started to open the animal up but then said 'I don't like this, it looks like anthrax.' So we had the vet out and sure enough it was anthrax and that closed you down, you couldn't move until you'd burnt it. I can remember digging this hole by hand, 2 or 3 of us there were no JCBs then. And it had to be filled with wood and straw and the carcass burnt and then all filled in.

There were quite a lot of cattle killed with lightning but it was the same as iyant, the carcass went black and there was a lot of waste - you couldn't use it and if they'd been stood a day or two they were no use anyway, so at that time a firm would take them away with the offal which was a different term for us than what butchers call offal.

Aubrey Boden had been with us for a while by the '47 winter; vehicles didn't run for 6 weeks - the roads around Thorncliffe were blocked solid. They kept trying to shift it with Big Mac things which cut and blew it but as fast as they did it, it blew back in. I never went to school for 6 weeks; the bus couldn't get. It normally came round by Meerbrook and picked me up last and at night I had to go round by Roche Grange and I was last off but I enjoyed the ride through the countryside.

Dad bought a horse as a knacker; he was about 14.2, thick set and half-legged. He had belonged to a coal merchant in Leek and he must have ill used him because he was thin as a rake when he came. I can remember him being fastened to the back of a wagon with hay on it and he was eating like mad. So we kept him and he just grew; we called him Smoky. We did hay carting with him and when Alec Brown, next door at Ankers Lane lost his horse, he borrowed him and Vic Steele borrowed him also.

In the '47 winter dad had a man working for him named Fred Bolton. He was a good joiner as well as lorry driving for us. Dad bought a lot of ammunition boxes after the war and Fred stripped them down and made sledges out of them. Dad took them to Jack Wests and they were sold. Then Fred made a big sledge for Smoky and we fetched cattle in from round Meerbrook with it. I can remember going with Aubrey up round Roche Grange. Aubrey must have used it for quite a while because we never had a wagon out for 6 weeks. Smoky turned out to be a very good asset to us.

There were two yaks on the Roches and various other animals but during that winter the bull yak died and we fetched it in; I think it was Aubrey fetched it. Dad saved the massive horns and the top of the head intending for them to be mounted outside the yard but it never got done. Afterwards I sometimes went up to the Roches on my bicycle to watch the cow yak with my dad's binoculars.

Before I was working for dad he had all this mill machinery, and any stuff that he couldn't sell over the counter, he put through the cooker and the 'whizz' and it was ground and separated into meat and bonemeal. There was a bone crusher first then a big steam boiler in what they called the meal place. There was all this shafting running off a big single cylinder Gardner Engine in the engine house. Then it went through the whizz which spun the fat out and then it was mill-ground and riddled and graded into different products like meat meal or meat and bonemeal which was then bagged up and sold. Some went for pig and poultry feed and some for fertilizer. We used to sell tallow; we put the liquid fat into 40 gallon drums, it went solid and we sold it to a firm, I guess it went for soap making. There wasn't a lot out of it; it was just a little extra.

By the time I started most of that had finished. He had intended to start canning pet food and had built the chimney with all the brickwork that carried a great horizontal boiler but I don't think smoke ever went up it, I think the council stopped it. He was going to call it 'Pussykin' and 'Wow'.

We used to skin sheep then and we had to salt the skins. If it was a cow hide you'd got to open it up and throw salt all over it; we had these big bags of salt. Then we had to wrap it up and stack them in a corner - they were heavy. The skin and hide man came for them about once a week.

Harry Mace had been with dad from early on and I used to go out with him, fetching in and he used to call at a pub for a drink; I had to sit in the wagon. I can remember sitting outside the Green Man at Bottomhouse for what seemed like hours. He never went anywhere without calling for a drink but was never drunk though. He worked for dad for 40 years.

Aubrey was a rum lad but a good, honest and reliable worker. Gordon went to live at Hulme End in a little cottage by the Light Railway pub and he walked from there in a morning. He'd occasionally get a lift with a quarry wagon; it was 9 miles and he got to work at 6.30 in a morning. If he saw a piece of timber by the road he'd carry it and leave it outside the door for me to cut up into logs. He walked in clogs, you could hear him coming. We had no electricity then so he had an old roadman's lamp with a wick in and he'd be cutting up using that. Then he'd walk back if he didn't get a lift. Now and then he'd go on the beer for 3 or 4 weeks at a time. If dad got desperate he'd go and fetch him then he wouldn't drink again for some time.

Eventually we had fridges but in the early stages when anything came in that had died it had to be disembowelled quickly. Anything that had died with the heat on it like grass staggers had to be done within an hour or two or it was spoiled.

I remember going to Mare Knowles, above Wincle, where James Brindley lived at one time, a really out of the way place. Mr Wainwright who was living there never drove and didn't have a phone. If he'd got something for us he'd walk to where he could catch a lift into Leek and up to the yard to tell us. Aubrey said he once went to pick up a cow and when he got there it was a stirk. 'I thought you said you'd got a cow Mr Wainwright.' He replied 'Aah, if they wants goo over yonder 'ill, there's a tu-three boons left over theer.' He hadn't told us about it early enough and foxes had been at it.

Colin and Family

But I went down this day with Joyce. I was always fascinated with countryside and we went in from Dumbers; there was no tower in those days. We drove along a rough road down the ridge and you could see Mare Knowles down below. You wouldn't have gone down in bad weather because you wouldn't have got back. I picked the beast up but he wanted to keep us. He was so glad to talk and made us so welcome.

Nowadays it's all changed of course and the farmer has to pay for animals to be disposed of; in some cases it's quite an amount. In those days we paid the farmer; everything had a use, nothing was wasted and nobody came to any harm. Mind you my mother was very particular. She was the daughter of Ralph de Tunstall Sneyd, a very gentle man. He wouldn't take kindly to anyone abusing animals and neither would she. If someone drove a cow up the yard with a stick on its final journey she would go out and put them in their place.

There was a lot of mauling and it was a dirty job, I wouldn't like to do it now. Circumstances finished it for me; my father died in 1954 and I had to go in National Service in 1955. Mother had to run the business and it was running down by the time I came home in 1957. There were too many middle men coming in then; a lot of thin cattle were bought for 'slink' butchers for pies. Mother said 'I can't keep it going.' So in 1958 Brassingtons took Easing Moor Farm out on lease.

Mother stayed in the house and they supplied her with water; they filled her tanks up from the borehole which my father had sunk in 1952. The agreement was that they took the yard on but they had got to keep Aubrey on and they'd got to keep Smoky. He lived till 1962 and then got down and died; mother wouldn't have him put down and when he died, no way was she having him sent to the yard. We had to bury him, John Ferns, my brother John, myself and Aubrey. Who'd have thought that of knacker people?

Mrs Wainwright, with her sons Fred and Hedley at Mare Knowles.

Bradnop Village c. 1950

A small village 4 miles from Leek on the Leek to Ashbourne Road, known as the Parish of Onecote cum Bradnop. Onecote Church was licensed for weddings and funerals but Bradnop parishioners had the use of the local school for Church of England services, the Vicar of Onecote officiating at Sunday services there. The village boasted not one but two Methodist chapels, both with healthy congregations in their early days. The Wesleyan Chapel is in the heart of the village adjacent to the old School and still a place of worship today. It was mainly run by the Needham family - Tom was the leader and Kathleen the organist. They were known as Uncle Tom and Aunty Kathleen to Sunday School scholars. Church children attended as well, in fact most village children attended, and went on trips to the seaside etc. There was a good turnout at the Anniversary with wooden staging erected, the youngest tots on the bottom row, the oldest on the top deck. The girls wore best white dresses and the boys white shirts. Tom and Kathleen gave a lifetime's service. Tom was loved by all of us and put many children on the correct path in life.

The Primitive Methodist Chapel was situated on the main Leek Road, but various factors forced it to close. It is now a private dwelling. The other focus in the village is the old school, known as Bradnop Parochial School, closed in 1978 for economic reasons. Bradnop had its own railway station at one time. When the line was closed coal was still delivered from there.

There was a public house called the Blacksmiths Arms on the main road at the junction with the village but this was burned down and remained a charred shell for many years until a private dwelling was built. I remember it clearly in the late 50s; we used to shelter there while waiting for the bus. The fire was reported to have been started upstairs by a cigarette. A small stone building alongside the pub was a wheelwright's shop and in between was the village forge, now a garage.

At the opposite end of the village past the railway station was a beautiful old house, Ashenhurst Hall. The Meiville family occupied it in the 1950s, although Mrs Meiville, a good friend and benefactor to the local school, was rarely seen. School children were told to be thankful to this mysterious lady for their Christmas presents that appeared out of Santa's sack each year.

The focus for all good things in the village centred around the school in the 1950s. Young and old looked forward to the two dances a year that took place, the Harvest Dance and the fancy dress Christmas dance both of which featured the Lancers, a lively and possibly quite dangerous activity in such a small place as laughing ladies were swung off their feet by enthusiastic gentlemen in the basket section of this dance. A good time was always had by all, and an opportunity not to be missed by young ladies and youths out 'talent spotting' - many a match was made in this place.

Bradnop schoolchildren on a nature walk near Middlecliffe 1961

Bradnop Schooldays. 1944-50

I remember my first day at school. The family had just moved into the village and we knew few people. I was wearing a brand-new red blazer and wore plaits. (My hair was not cut properly until I was 13 when Mum was fed up drying my thick, curly hair in front of the old black-lead grate). The teacher was Miss Jenny Mears who greeted me at the door and said how very beautiful my blazer was and I felt very proud and special. What a kind introduction to the unknown. The other teacher was Mrs Clare Clowes, who smoked and wore lipstick, quite shocking to us at the time. I loved her because she told us such marvellous stories at the end of the day, nearly always a cliffhanger, and I could hardly wait to hear the next instalment. This was good training for my adult life as a teacher - I developed various strategies to keep my listeners attentive and excited.

I must have been a very average scholar because my work never seemed to be displayed on the partition walls that separated the infants and junior classes. But on one memorable occasion my potato print was on show and I was thrilled to bits. I was always a good reader but poor at maths. It was, and still is, a bit of a nightmare and Miss Mears kept me in on many occasions while I wrestled with the jumble on the blackboard. She usually told me the answer in the end, probably to get rid of me I suspect. We sang hymns and songs unaccompanied and gruffly. My other dread was needlework, always ending up at the teacher's desk with a jumble of stitches and threads.

PE or 'Drill' as it was called took place on the stony playground. We were divided into four teams, red, green, blue and yellow. We wore coloured bands during exercise and games. I was in the yellow team which always seemed to be the last on the colour chart on the classroom wall. Red was always winning and I was quite jealous. We had formal handwriting lessons with pen and ink. Mavis Eardley was the ink monitor and I always wanted her job. Her handwriting was beautiful.

In the days before hot lunches we took sandwiches to school. Miss Mears always had hot milk with her lunch, boiling it up on a little stove. We thought it very odd! Michael Birch once swopped his thick chunk of slab cake for a fancy cake out of her lunchbox when she went to the outside toilet. He really thought that she would not notice but we waited with much nervous anticipation to see what would happen. To her credit she stayed expressionless and dignified, saying nothing but she told my mother about it later and they had a good laugh. Michael was always being silly. He once told her that he had eaten 17 pancakes on Shrove Tuesday and she told him off for fibbing. Another memorable episode was when John Titterton kicked Miss Mears on the shins because he would not change his hobnailed boots for his indoor shoes. He terrified the life out of us.

My recollections of Bradnop School are a little sketchy but I have fond memories of two wonderful teachers, patient and kind, who fostered a love of reading and excellence at spelling which stood me in good stead for the future. It may have been small and cramped but the education I received was the best in the world. I left with sadness but excitement too and most of all, affection and gratitude for time well spent there.

We lived at Golden farm which was built in 1806 as the Vicarage for Onecote cum Bradnop Parish and used as such until 1866 when Onecote vicarage was built. My mother was caretaker at the school cum church and I was her little helper and so Friday night after school was busy; there was the schoolroom to sweep and dust, outside toilets to clean and furniture to polish but worst of all was the boiler to clean out and stoke up. Down the dangerous stone steps into the gloom and choking fumes, down into the bowels of the earth! Mother would descend with me in tow into this black pit lit by the smallest of light bulbs. Sometimes the fire would be out - horror! Mother would be cursing under her breath and scratching frantically at the thick lumps of clinker with a

Bradnop school children 1952.
Back: Miss Clowes, Ted Williams, Vernon Egerton, Joe Bowyer. Stan Heath, Fred Gee, Ralph Robinson.
2: George Torr, Geoff Sillito, Margaret Torr, Freda Hine, Doreen Simcock, Ann Barks, Philip Egerton, Miss Mears
3: Marion Heath, Joan Clulow, Sylvia Needham, Christine Bowyer, Doreen Needham, Elizabeth Truman, Marion Sales, Pat Lovenbury, Sheila Needham.
Front row: Peter Tompkinson, Basil Bagshaw, David Wheeldon, Robin Lichfield, Eric Torr, David Gee, John Egerton, Edmund Hine.

Bradnop School Feb 1960

Bradnop School c.1960.

BELOW
Harold Bode,
headmaster in 1965.

long handled rake. Occasionally if the fire would not relight, no matter what, there was only one thing to do, swallow your pride and send for neighbour Sid. Soon the fire would be drawing well and Mother would be content again.

Each Friday we had to change over from school to church for the Sunday afternoon service. Stack the children's desks and chairs, drag the pulpit and lectern out of the cloakroom, push them into their places, heavy and unwieldy things! The altar to set up and remember which coloured embroidered drapes to get out, the crisp white lace cloth must be smoothed down with loving care; fit to receive the sacred cross in its middle. Line up a dozen chairs, straight and true and don't forget a hymn book AND a prayer book for each chair.

Then after the service as the vicar retires to the tiny room at the back, a small respectful wait until the heavy door clangs shut then, 'Quick Barbara, collect up all the books.' Stack the chairs, drag the furniture back into the cloakroom, puffing and panting. Take down the beautiful embroidery and the altar cloth and wrap carefully in tissue. What to do with the altar flowers? One last look round then down into the boiler house - yes, the fire is in. Alleluia! And all for half a crown an hour.   Barbara Rogers

Bradnop 1978
Back: Derek Torr, Nigel Nicholls, Doreen Needham, Margaret Torr, David Wheeldon, David Gee
Standing: Ralph Robinson, Joan Clulow, Doreen Simcock, Sheila Needham, Olive Gee, Vera Gee,
Malcolm Needham, Raymond Needham, Maurice Torr.
Seated: Edith Clark, Dorothy Sheldon, Kathleen Eardley, Mavis Eardley, Barbara Blore.
Front: Winifred & Sylvia Needham.

On Bradnop School
Green 22-1-1958

Confirmation at Onecote (Onecote cum Bradnop), including:
Frank Eardley, John Turnock, Tom Goldstraw, Wilmot Turnock, Ernest Goldstraw,
Raymond Turnock, Jeffrey Blore, Gwen Beardmore, Linda Bainbridge, Dorothy Smith,
Hilda Beardmore, Frances Bainbridge, Mavis Eardley, Barbara Blore.

Mavis Bailey

I was born at Middlecliffe Farm, Bradnop on June 1st 1936 and started at Bradnop School when I was five years old. I can't remember how many children were in the school, but we were all in one big classroom - all different ages, apart from when those who were due to sit the 11 plus exam went to one end of the room and a big partition was pulled across, so that they could study in a quieter space. Miss Mears taught all the different subjects to different age groups. As far as I can recall no-one left the school being unable to read, write, or understand maths (or sums as we called them then) - what a change from today!! We had 12 long pieces of card with the times tables written on them from 1x1 up to 1x12. They hung on nails on the wall and we learnt to recite each one perfectly.

In the summer when we had lovely sunny weather, Miss Mears would get all the bigger children to carry the desks and chairs out into the little playground next to Charlie Mycock's field and the small children would take their books and pencils etc. outside. She would try to make sure that we each had a hat on to guard against the sun and so we happily sat outside to do our lessons - we loved those days. On other nice days she would take us for a nature walk around the lanes near the school where we would pick wild flowers and leaves, which we took back to the classroom to put into scrapbooks to press and write their names underneath.

At break time we would line up and the milk monitors would give each one of us a little half-pint bottle of milk which they had collected earlier from Mr & Mrs Doody's farm opposite the school. I loved my time as a milk monitor and felt quite important being allowed to cross the road and bring back the correct amount of milk. We always had a laugh with Mrs Doody who was a jolly little lady. At the end of the school day a group of us who lived towards Ashenhurst would walk home together having lots of fun on the way. There were the two Needham twins, Sylvia and Winifred, Margaret Johnson, John Titterton, Michael and Delilah Gough and myself. Each Christmas, for a few years, Miss Mieville from Ashenhurst Hall would give all the schoolchildren a gift - sometimes it would be one of her own or her mother's own personal possessions. I have still got a lovely locket she gave me one year. Miss Mears was a dedicated, caring teacher whom we all loved and greatly respected and I, for one, was very sad to leave such a happy, secure environment.

When Rene and I were younger we went to Sunday school at the Primitive Chapel near to Oxhay where once a year we had the Anniversary Service. The girls wore lovely white dresses and the boys wore white shirts and dark trousers and we all sat on tiered wooden forms covered with white material and sang songs to our audience (we always dreaded being asked to do a solo!) As we got older we went with our Mum and Dad to both the Church and Chapel services. Rene sometimes played the organ at the Church service which was held in the schoolroom and was led by the Onecote-cum-Bradnop Vicar.

I have happy memories of the dances that were held in the schoolroom when Vic Alcock and his band came to play and everyone let their hair down doing the Gay Gordons and the Lancers amongst many other dances. I remember clearly (and with much embarrassment at the time) how my Dad would position himself by the door at the end of the evening in order to ensure that neither Rene or myself sneaked off with some young man who wanted to take us home! Whist Drives were also held in the schoolroom, which were always well attended, but I never got the hang of the game and so wasn't very interested. I just went to watch and help with the refreshments.

A very vivid memory of my time at Bradnop was when there was a heavy fall on snow in

Bradnop near the
Stocks Tree

Stile House Lane Feb 1958

Ashbourne Road
25-2-58

1947 which seemed to last for ages. All the roads out of Leek were blocked with massive drifts, making it impossible for even the snow-ploughs to get through. The only way the roads could be opened was by gangs of men trying to clear them by hand digging which as you can imagine by the distance to be done took ages. We were fast in at our farm for about six weeks. My Dad made quite a number of journeys during that time walking on top of the drifts into Leek to bring back food and about a dozen loaves of bread in corn sacks which my Mum had washed.

When the snow was at its heaviest I remember us drawing the curtains back and realising that we couldn't see the downstairs windows of Hine's farm opposite as the snowdrifts were so high. Dad had to climb out through our bedroom window, walk across the top of the snowdrifts then slowly begin to dig a way down through it to get to the shippon, where the cows were, so that he could feed and milk them. The next day after more digging he managed to get Bonnie our horse out of her stable and an old sledge from in there, attaching Bonnie to it and lifting the milk churns on it hoping to get the milk up to the main road, going across the fields, over the railway lines and through Mrs Keeling's farm at Wylde Goose. This proved useless as Bonnie got stuck in the snowdrifts and had to be dug out. I was watching through the bedroom window and ended up crying and shouting at Dad to leave her alone. We didn't manage to get the milk away for a while and had to resort to pouring what milk we didn't require down the grid at the bottom of the shippon. We eventually did get out when the lanes were freed by hand-digging by teams of men.

I left Bradnop to live in Leek with my parents when Dad retired from farming in 1959. I have always loved living in Leek but I still have a very soft spot in my heart for Bradnop.

Toll House Petrol Station on Ashbourne Road c.1960

Cyril Warrington

My mother was born and raised at Middlecliffe Farm, part of the Ashenhurst estate; she married in 1928. In 1934 my parents, Joseph Warrington and Florence Matilda (née Clarke), moved to the Revedge Farm, also part of the Ashenhurst estate. I was 3 years old at the time.

The estate was owned by Mrs Phillips, widow of General Philips who passed away in 1913. The Revedge Farm, one of many farms on the estate, was situated close to Ashenhurst Hall. The farm had 100 acres of land and the annual rent was £120, paid half yearly at the Hall.

I started school at 5 years of age in 1936. The school was 1^1/2 miles walk from the Revedge Farm and my brother John and I would often encounter Mrs Phillips as we were walking home. Mrs Phillips was a very gracious lady and seemed to be fond of children as she would often stop and talk to us. On many occasions she would give us a Foxes glacier mint or if she was in her chauffeur driven car she would give us a new penny. I remember her car very well; it was a maroon Classic Standard car, highly polished, of course! On one occasion, at Christmas, Mrs Phillips even gave my brother and myself a scarf each that she had taken the trouble to knit. We have very fond memories of her.

Part of the estate was sold around 1940 and the Revedge Farm made £1750. The rest of the estate farms were sold later. We continued to live at the farm until 1947 under a new landlord. Ashenhurst Hall was demolished in 1954, the year I was married.

Bradnop Station 1952. *Courtesy J. Morten*

Raymond Needham

I used to live at Holly House Farm. The winters were very bad and the road from Moss Rose to Bradnop was always blocked by snow. The photograph shows our lane being dug out in 1963 by John Needham, my father, Archie Day and myself. In 1947 my father sledged the milk down the fields to Bradnop Toll Bar for seven weeks. I don't remember a lot about it as I was only six years old then. Also Mr Finney from Lark Hall Farm died and was kept in the house until the funeral. The road was dug out the day before the funeral only to become blocked again the next day. They put the coffin on a sledge and took it down the fields to the waiting hearse. In comparison the summers were usually good. You can see us in the photographs getting the hay in as in those days silage was not made.

Derek Torr

I was born and brought up at Cliff Head Farm, Bradnop along with my two brothers George and Maurice. We had no electric until the late 1950s and I remember well all five of our family handmilking the herd of 18 to 20 cows; I learned to milk as a five year old; you were started on some cow that was nice and quiet so you could put the bucket on the floor because you weren't strong enough to hold it between your legs. We all had our own little milking stool and I've had many a time when the cow kicked and put you, your bucket and your stool into the groop. You had to milk your own quota of cows before going to school and anything a bit hard or lively was left to mum and dad. You went with your lanterns to give some light and it was a grand warm job in cold weather but in mid summer when you'd been getting some hay and they'd got flies nipping, you got whisked round the ears and in the face with dirty tails!

The evening's milk was sieved into 12 gallon churns and stood in a trough of flowing cold water overnight and the morning's milk was poured down a fridge on a stand in the house to cool it and then the churns were bowled down the passage and out onto the milk stand where they were picked up by Hodgkiss Dairies.

Abberleys from Rudyard came round with a grocery van once a week and meat was delivered to one of the farms on the main road on a Saturday after being ordered on Wednesday when going to market. We picked ours up from Throstles Nest ready for our Sunday roast. And I remember the 'Bagman' coming; it was Bill Shemilt from Ipstones. He bought our empty corn sacks for a few pence each.

In the winter of 1947 the main road was closed for 6 weeks; I remember a bus being blocked in for that time across from the farm. Milk was taken by horse and sledge down to Bradnop cross roads where it was open - that was the gathering place where provisions could be picked up too.

We never went to school for 6 weeks either. In summer if it was nice weather we went for a walk from school down to Ashenhurst Hall where we were given a drink on the lawn. Mrs Meiville the owner used to give the schoolchildren presents at Christmas and used to come and give them out at a party in school.

Other recollections are of our family walking down the fields, over the brook and up the other side to Bradnop Primitive Methodist Chapel. The Torr families of Cliff Head and Middle Cliff would have been the main sponsors when the chapel was built in 1889 and we were always involved until the chapel closed in 1970. It was a simple room with a little entrance porch inside. There were nice wooden pews and it was heated by an old stove which you had to go down steps to light and if the wind was in the wrong direction the chapel would fill with smoke. Dad used to light the fire and the four hanging lamps; there was no electricity until about 1960. As kids when we got big enough we could put blow bellows up through the hole in the middle of them to blow them out at night.

In the late '40s and '50s everyone walked to chapel; there was a service every Sunday and at times on a weekday night, and Sunday school was every Sunday morning at 11 o'clock with an attendance of up to 30. Vernon Egerton was Superintendent and teachers were father - Clifford Torr, Uncle Jim Torr and Mrs Birch. Vernon organised the Chapel Anniversary in May and a trip out in summer. He was quite good with kids but could be a bit strict and do a bit of shouting. We also attended Club Day when the Market Place in Leek was crammed full.

Mother was the organist. In autumn were two services for harvest and the harvest sale. Enza Titterton from Coltsmoor conducted the sale; he also did Thorncliffe and Bradnop Wesleyan.

When he died Arthur Clowes did it for a while and Jack Tatton but we used to get home about half past 11 when he did it. I took over until the chapel closed.

The Wesleyans and 'Prims' only went to each other's special services; there were services at both chapels each Sunday evening. The chapels were in different circuits; we were under Bethesda in Leek. Uncle Jim was a preacher in the 'Prim' circuit and could be going out to Cellarhead or Newstone behind the Roches or Morridge End.

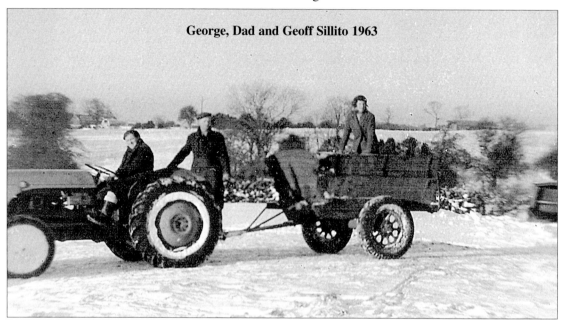

George, Dad and Geoff Sillito 1963

Clifford Torr, Betty Allen (Land girl), with Torr lads and Betty's nephew

CLIFF HEAD FARM

George, Maurice & Derek 1959

Clifford Torr & Bill Sillito

Left: Derek 1961

Thelma Ferns

My father was called Gordon Adolphus Francis Eric
Corbishley; why Adolphus I don't know. He was an only child
and a builder and 'jack of all trades'. My granddad was a
farmer and I think they moved quite a few times; they used to
reckon that my grandma Rosie never unpacked from one place
to another. They had some land on Folly Lane at Cheddleton;
there is a large house on the left which dad built and lived at
and he built a row of bungalows which he let out and then built
another larger house further down when he got married to
mum, Nellie Tomlinson. Dad could put his hand to anything
and worked very hard.

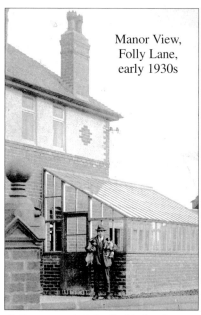

Manor View,
Folly Lane,
early 1930s

Dad and his parents had kept the Red Lion at Thorncliffe
in 1901 and in 1941 we came from Cheddleton to it again
when dad took the tenancy. It belonged to Mr Argles who
owned a lot of property round here.

I was 7 years old and can remember as evening came and they wanted to light the lamps
hanging on the walls. The lamps had glass shades and every one had been drained of paraffin; the
outgoing tenant had emptied the lot so we had to have candles. The funny thing was we did end
up selling paraffin from the pub. It wasn't a very good combination was it, beer and paraffin. It
used to come in drums and you turned a tap to get a gallon out and folks used to come with a can.
It was on the backyard and easier for people from the village to fetch because there was no electric
then. Eventually we had a generator.

We were milking 60 cows at the Red Lion as well. We all did it; I milked with a three legged
stool and dad employed quite a lot of people from the village. There weren't many who had
transport and we were the first to have a telephone. The residents would give our number and we
had to run to and fro with messages.

With having all these cattle dad would go to the brewery in the Potteries; I think it was
Burslem. We had off Norris's Brewery and Parker's Brewery and there was always brewers grains
so he used to load the lorry up to the top of the side boards with grains and then load the barrels
of beer on the top; just drop them into the grains.

We used to make cheese; we all took
part. We got the churn and lifted it into the
old copper boiler until it got to the correct
temperature then put the rennet in and
then we had a big round blue vat where
the curds were tipped in and after it had
settled you started cutting it then you had
rings with a cheesecloth in which were
filled and put under the cheese press.
There was a spare bedroom to store them
in and then dad used to sell the cheese.

Gordon Jnr, Tony &
Thelma at the Red Lion,
Thorncliffe, late 1940s.

Then the Yanks appeared on the
scene and it was a very busy place. They

used to come up the valley from Blackshaw Camp not round by the road. I used to plonk on the piano; they were always singing and one they sang over and over again was Red River Valley. I can remember it today.

The pub came up for sale and they bought it and he bought Lower Farm in Thorncliffe and my grandma came living there. We went to the school which was also the church which was run from St Luke's in Leek. There was a partition in and an organ. I was confirmed there.

Joe Peacock was at Underbank and when we were at school he used to bring the milk across in little bottles for the children. Mrs Dick Williams did the dinners; they came from town and she had a paraffin stove to keep them warm. There was also a library run from the school in a big cupboard.

We used to go to Sunday school at the chapel; Amy Dale played the organ. There was a large family of Clowes at Coplowe; I think Mrs Clowes had 12 children. Granny Clowes lived on the corner with her sister Miss Bowyer; two old ladies.

Dad kept a mixture of cattle then he bought Highfield Home farm and Highfield Stud Farm and had all Friesians up there and then he bought Home farm at Consall and he was sending 1000 gallons of milk a day off all the farms. He also kept pigs at Highfield and Aubrey Boden and Joe Lancaster worked for him there. They

Above: 1960

Gordon Corbishley, Red Lion Thorncliffe 1950

also reared their own pigs up there. (on dad's feed) He was in a big way; he was always doing something. He had done the pub up and employed a Polish man who had come to Blackshaw Moor.

He went off in the cattle wagon to Shrewsbury Market one day and had a stroke. My brother managed to get him in the lorry and bought him home then we had a blizzard and my brother Gordon had to go with a tractor to meet the doctor, John Watson, who came back with him on the tractor. The doctor said he'd worn himself out; I came home but he died three weeks later - he was only 54.

Thorncliffe Chapel at Club Day c.1950 Mabel & Irene Williams, Brenda Grindey, Thelma Corbishley.

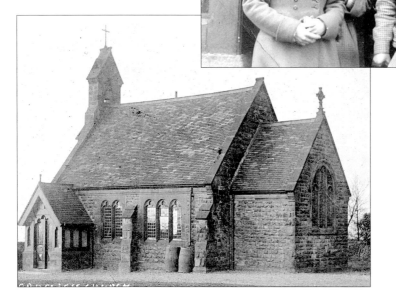

Coronation Day 1953 at Thorncliffe Church. Irene & Edith Williams, Roy Leech, Brenda Grindey, Freda Clowes, Mabel Williams.

Thorncliffe Church and School.

Thorncliffe School 1925

Back L–R: Victor Rider, Elsie Clowes, Harriet Pickford, Myrtle Tunnicliffe, Jack Howell, Arthur Clowes, Claude Tunnicliffe, John Oulsnam, Victor Brunt, Raymond Clowes, Ethel Goldstraw, Cissie Barks -- --, Mr Howson (Governor).

Next Row: -- --, -- --, -- --, Dora Hine, -- --, Maud Hine, Vinnie Barks, Emma Clowes, Margaret Felthouse, Alice Felthouse, Phyllis Clewlow, Mary Howell, -- --.

Second Row: -- --, Eddie Clowes, Alice Prince (teacher), Sam Bennison, -- --, Alice Williams, -- --, Miss Bradley (teacher), Elsie Hine, George Barks, Harriet Barks.

Front: -- --, Ted Williams, Billy Gilman, -- --, -- --, -- --, George Oulsnam, Isaac Pickford, Jim Bennison, Joe Lancaster, George Barks

Thorncliffe School 1925

Smithy Cottage, Thorncliffe. Granny Clowes.

Ashes Farm, Thorncliffe, possibly the Critchlows. It used to be known as Little Easing.

Red Lion, Thorncliffe

Bottom of Thorncliffe Bank.

1947 Poles digging out Thorncliffe Lane.

Thorncliffe Chapel late 1940s. Preacher George Lowe is back left, Stanley Buxton is back centre.

Thorncliffe Chapel 1950.
Back: Minnie Clowes, Mrs Buxton, Kath Dale (Gee)
2: Joan Grindey, Kath Clowes, Christine Grindey, May Clowes, - -, June Clowes
3: Malcolm Clowes, - Edgar, Mary Stevenson, Joe Barks, - Edgar, Shirley Boden, Alan Barks
4: Margaret Stevenson, Rosalyn Gould, Susan Carding, Christine Barks, 2 x Bodens, Barbara Gould, Gail Clowes

Thorncliffe School 1960s. Mr Morris & Mrs Owen.
Back: Les Needham, Peter Gilman, William Ferns, --, Neil Ferns, --, --, --,
Mick Day, Ian Barks, John Gilman, Janet Day, Julie Shenton, Sheila Needham, Pat Glover, --, Yvonne Shenton

Wallhill at Bottom of Broad Street c.1912

C.1938

Jean Hulme: Colin, Gentleman of the Road

Colin

I used to say Colin wasn't a tramp but a Gentlcman of the Road. He wouldn't hurt anybody; he was an intelligent man but very frightened - I think he was shell-shocked from the war. He lived on Warslow Common. There was a lot of snow and nobody had seen him in Leek so we took him some food up and warm socks.

He lived in a dugout in a bank side with zinc tins for a roof and bags hanging down the front. There was a brook in the bottom where he got his water and holes dug out in the ground with saucepans in which contained his food. He'd got a little round stove which he'd got from one of the army huts. It's a wonder the smoke didn't kill him; that's why he was so black.

I shouted,'Colin, Are you in?' There's some food.' When he knew it was us, he came out. We started to walk back up the common to get some milk but he couldn't walk - he'd got no shoes only plastic bags so in the snow they were slipping everywhere.

Sometimes he went in the Herbage barn in winter and in the big shed where there were cows and hay. Joe said, 'You can go in but you can't smoke in there.' He once had a sore on his chest and I said, 'You need to see a doctor.' He said, 'It's all right.' And he put a maggot in it, which cured it. I think he'd been in a survival unit in the war.

He used to sit on the seat at the Moss Rose and when I went past I gave him some milk from our milk round. He always carried a bag and I said, 'What have you got in it?' He opened it and there were a lot of bottle tops which he put in his bed for drainage with bags on top. And I said 'You've got more food in here than I have in my pantry.' Shops used to put stuff out for him that was going out of date so it didn't look like he was pinching it.

I asked round for some big boots for him and a police inspector got me a new pair of wellingtons and the next time I saw Colin he'd cut off the front of the toes!

When he couldn't manage the walk back to the moor he lived in a barn at Thorncliffe. People in Leek were so good with him and at his funeral at St Lukes, the church was packed.

Far left, Mr Sigley.
Mr Frank Green, Leek Health Inspector
at the entrance to the Park, Vicarage Road.

BURN REFUSE, SAVE RATES.

Taking the milk from W. Turnocks, Meerbrook, in a bad winter

RURAL SCENES

Mr & Mrs Goodall at Horton, snowridding.

BELOW
Old John West after the shoot at Whiston or Ipstones where they had land. He took over the long established Wooliscrofts hardware store in Leek, which became the well-known firm of J. West & Son also supplying agricultural implements, etc to the faming community (it closed about 1980.)

Gordon Roberts

I was born in Liverpool in 1931. My father, Bob Roberts was a marine engineer; he was also born in Liverpool where his father was a coalman. He had a shire horse that pulled the cart; I can remember when I was about 4 years old he plonked me on the shire's back while he delivered the coal and I sat there with my legs stuck out sideways because his back was so broad. I enjoyed that.

Gordon

My mother, Irene Cartwright was born in Leek, the youngest daughter of John Cartwright who was a bank clerk at the District Bank in Derby Street. She too became a bank clerk but decided that she would be more useful to her country as a nurse in the event of another war and so went to Liverpool Royal Infirmary in 1919. She became a Theatre Sister for a famous surgeon named Blair-Bell and while she was there a sailor came in with appendicitis and that was the start of my parent's relationship. They married in 1927 and went on to have 5 children.

While growing up, we children and mother saw very little of my father; he would only appear at home for a week or two, once or twice a year. Once he was at sea for three years before his ship came home; hence the gap of four years between me and my younger sister. I remember the excitement his home coming caused. My elder sister, mother and I went down to the docks in the tram car to greet him; it was a great day.

We lived in a house with gas lighting, linoleum floors and rag rugs. The war was coming so in 1939 they decided to come to Leek because they thought Liverpool might be bombed - which it was. So in April we settled in to Dampier Street. They had paid £400 for a house in Liverpool and had to pay £600 for a house in Leek; it was a big step up for them. Father was on the Atlantic for much of the 2nd World War.

My maternal grandmother, born Anne Wooliscroft, lived with her husband, John Cartwright nearby in Spencer Avenue and in the same street around 1940 appeared Edwin Hodgkinson, a Veterinary Surgeon. (Qualified 1939) He'd come up the road in his car and skid to a halt outside his garage door several times a day. I thought he must have an interesting life - he's always out.

Our parents purchased 3 bicycles for their 3 oldest children which were much appreciated and put to good use. Having realised that I preferred being out doors to sitting in the classroom and also that schooldays would not last for ever I asked Mr Hodgkinson 'Please can I come and see what you're doing?' What is known as 'seeing practice.' He said 'Yes' and I enjoyed it. I spent some time making 'Flat Powders' stomach powders for cows. There were 5 or 6 ingredients, including something that made them smell nice, and bicarb. It was all mixed up in big bowl and then measured out onto papers which had to be folded up a special way. There were 6 in a packet which sold for 5 bob. I also made Aperient Powders - magnesium sulphate for stoppages. There was also FPQ fever prevention, and all sorts of bottles: liniment with a cross on top, Potassium Iodide which would cure wooden tongue and disinfectant which was called PL (pink lotion). There were no antibiotics in those days.

So I worked hard at school and got my school certificate in 1946 and then my Higher School Certificate in 1948 and had a 2nd go in 1949 for better results. (But no better) Then I applied to get into University to try and become a vet. Those were the days when they were taking in ex-servicemen and I hadn't done my 2 years national Military Service. I had already had my army medical and failed. I had gone to Hanley where there were about 60 lads. After the preliminaries we went into the gymnasium where there were some dozen doctors. We were told to strip off and when I got to the 2nd one he said 'Bend over.' And he grabbed my buttocks to see if I'd got piles and then he said 'Cough.' This gave me quite a shock. He said 'Right, on to the next.' This was a heart specialist. He listened to my ticker which was pounding away with shock. He said 'Eh, come and listen to this one.' So his comrades came and listened and said 'Oh, we don't like that.' So I was sent to a heart specialist, an elderly man with somewhat ancient equipment, who agreed with the doctors, classified me as Grade 4 - no swimming, no sports and with luck I might make the age of 50.

Arriving home on the bus, having not as usual offered my seat to an elderly lady, (I had a bad heart) I was somewhat subdued. Mother said 'What's up?' I told her and she didn't say anything but then a fortnight later she told me that we were going for a second opinion which we did.

'Nothing wrong with your heart.' He said after a thorough examination. 'It is just a bit bigger than normal - carry on with life.' Mother and I decided to accept this opinion. I am very pleased that my mother had been a nurse and knew that I had led a normal life and decided on this second opinion.

I wrote to Liverpool; this was the only University that would even consider my application, London and Bristol said no - Glasgow and Edinburgh were for Scots' only and the same with Dublin. I said 'I can come now.' 'No.' They said 'You'll have to wait 2 years until you are the same age as those who have done military service.' So I thought I'll go farm labouring and learn a bit about animals. First I went to Impney Farm near Worcester for a year; a mixed farm with beef cattle, pigs and poultry. A lot of hand work loading muck and carrying pig corn on your back in sacks and handling many tons of potatoes. The pigs once knocked me over and grabbed the corn off me which was one lesson learnt.

We could be working all night to get the crops sown; perhaps planting potatoes in the 50 acre field. It seemed as big as the universe to me, this 50 acre field. I was sent up there with a hoe to weed. I did two rows and thought 'It will take me the rest of the year to do it all.' They got some casual labour in to do the potato harvesting; about 20 housewives from Droitwich on a trailer behind the tractor.

Next I went to work for Mr Johnson of Mixon Hay. I was picked up by lorry along with two builders, two carpenters and two or three farm labourers; some were elderly, I was the youngest. I often worked with Percy the horseman. One day we shifted 20 loads of muck by hand, taking it off with 2 horses and a flat cart and spreading it by hand.

So in 1951 I started at the Faculty of Veterinary Science at Liverpool University. After 4 years, the final year was at Lea Hurst on the Wirral; a large animal place with farms attached. We were doing operations several times a week on horses and caesareans on cows, all sorts and old hat nowadays.

They taught me to castrate a big boar. 'You do it,

1956, newly qualified, with his landlady Mrs Dutton.

Roberts.' He was fastened up by a noose round his nose. I gave him an overdose of barbiturates injected straight into his testicles. After a while he went drowsy and lay down to sleep. I tweaked his ears - no response, so scrubbed him up and castrated him but of course in the process removed the anaesthetic so he was able to start his recovery.

In July 1956 I was a qualified vet and for 18 months I went to work for Bobby Pritchard, a vet from Denbigh. A lot of welsh ewes came in to be lambed and as Bobby was a big man, he couldn't bend or squat easily so he used to have his ewes held by the back legs and lamb them upside down whereas I would have them lying down in their natural position. He had an assistant, Ifor Davies who at 89 was still working. He was so kind and gentle and I learned more about lambing sheep from him than ever I learned at college.

Edwin Hodgkinson got in touch saying there was a job for me in Leek and offering £200 more than Bobby Pritchard and so I came back. The practice had been owned by Hector Macintyre. He had come to Leek in 1918 after qualifying in Glasgow; he thought he would make more money coming south. Things were very different then; he started work on horseback with a horseman, Jimmy to look after it. He had no telephone - if you wanted a vet you sent a lad or someone with a message. Later he had a motorbike and then a car. When I knew him he was plump and elderly and looked over his glasses at you.

I remember him when antibiotics were being introduced. It was the only time I ever saw practice with Mac, this one trip. He was given a syringe and a bottle of penicillin by Emrys Bowen and instructions to inject. Emrys was a young working vet while Mac was an old fashioned one who'd possibly never given an injection and who knew nothing about these new fangled drugs. He was muttering to himself as he drove, '10cc out of this bottle and stick it in the cow.' It was probably a case of streptococcal mastitis which responded instantly.

Edwin had come from Uttoxeter where his father was a chemist. He was a partner with Mac after 6 years. It was 16 years before I became a partner. Michael Davies and Geddys Thompson were there when I started, replaced by Derek Callander who went on to become DVO for Kent and Surrey in charge of control of Rabies.

One of the worst things when I was practising was Anthrax; we saw more in the early years

NFU Dinner 1956-57. Recently retired vet, Mr H McIntyre and his wife standing behind Mr & Mrs J Winterton, Mr T.H. Ball to left, Mr & Mrs H. Mear to right of Wintertons.

which we blamed on imported feed from India in particular. I remember one story about two farmers in wartime; one found a cow dead unexpectedly so asked his neighbour to come and help dress the cow and see if they could sell the meat. As they were doing it, they pulled out a big swollen spleen. One said 'I don't like the look of that.' 'Why?' said the other. 'Well, they reckon it's Anthrax.' They'd got blood splattered down them so they called the vet and Emrys went along and examined a blood smear. 'Yes, it's Anthrax - I'd go and see a doctor if I were you.'

So they went to see John Watson who had a reputation in Leek. They went in looking scared. 'Well?' says JW. So they told him about the dead cow and that Emrys had advised them to see a doctor. 'WELL, BUGGER OFF AND COME BACK WHEN YOU'VE GOT IT!' was the reply. Luckily they didn't get it.

When you looked on the slide you saw black rods with a reddish capsule around them. We used a particular stain called Methylene Blue. When you'd seen a few samples, which we did in our student days under the microscope, you didn't forget a black rod in a red jacket. You could soon be a dead man if it got into your circulation.

Another thing which we don't see now is warbles. I remember seeing a 6 month old calf in Wales which hadn't thrived; it was skin and bone and as he moved his back went squeak, squeak. He'd got all these holes containing a big fat maggot waiting to come out; there must have been several dozen. He had to be knackered.

When I qualified, to anaesthetise a cat we had a jam jar with cotton wool and a splash of ether and you put the cats head in. If it needed a bit more, you pushed its head further in and if its breathing slowed too much, you pulled it out.

Sometimes things could be quite dramatic; I remember being called out to a milk fever one summer morning. Half way there and a torrential down pour commenced; at first it was of large hail-stones, as big as walnuts but by the time we reached the farm the hail had turned to torrential rain. Alan lurched out of the darkness, dressed in foul weather gear; a sou'wester and a sack bag draped around the shoulders of his coat. 'We'll have to be quick,' he cried, 'She'll be washed away!'

I put on my parturition gown, Scottie, my assistant had on my rubber coat, not having any waterproof clothing with him. It had after all been a normal summer morning when he had set off to see a days practice.

Pausing only to gather up two bottles of calcium, and a flutter valve injection apparatus, we set off, on foot, through the storm. Alan shouting, his face streaming with rain water periodically illuminated by lightning flashes, that his cow had come to rest in the bottom of a gully, on the far side of the sloping field which we were crossing. Normally the gully was dry, but not now; there was a powerful stream roaring down it, threatening to wash Alan's cow away.

It remained dark, the thunder roared, the lightning blinded us, the deluge was continuous. Conversation was difficult; it came in short bursts, shouted, and at close range. Alan led us to his cow; she was in a gully about twenty feet deep with extremely steep sides. The bottom of the gully sloped down the field, towards the main road, and down it ran, at considerable speed, a river of brown water, a foot to eighteen inches deep. Fortunately the cow was lying on a sort of shelf to one side, in no more than four inches of water.

Standing in the side of the torrent, the jugular vein was found, the needle was inserted, the flutter valve attached and the calcium administered by raising the bottle in the air. I felt more like a lightning conductor than usual in this storm. Scottie offered, but I couldn't give him the bottle; he was younger than I was - more life in front of him. I always felt very exposed in a thunderstorm,

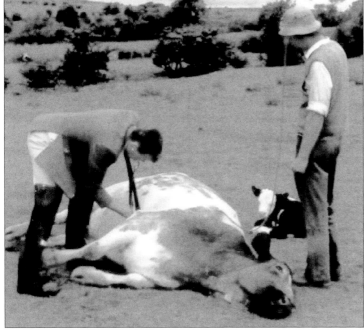

Treating milk fever at Lower Elkstone.

standing there wet through, with one arm raised to the heavens.

The first bottle finished, we gave her the second under her skin to last her. Alan asked, 'What happens if the water rises higher?' With the storm continuing vigorously, I hoped, very earnestly, that this cow would be one of those that rose more or less immediately, having received the requisite dose of calcium. She was; she not only rose, but set off, tottering, up the side of the gully, with me holding on to the base of her tail, providing uplift, a steady push, and a counter effect to her swaying, plus gentle verbal encouragement.

'Come on old girl, you can do it!' Towards the top she helped me, pulling me up out of the gully. Arriving at the top I released her tail, and she disappeared into the storm.

'She'll be all right now, Alan.'

We towelled off, washed up, drank a cup of tea and departed. The storm was lessening, the sky was getting lighter; it wasn't long before we were in sunshine again.

In my time I saw many cattle which had been struck by lightning, and many more which might have been. Sometimes one could see burn marks on the skin, usually running from the spine. Those were direct strikes. Sometimes, on post mortem examination no signs of any sort were to be detected, by my eyes at least. In those cases ones diagnosis needed to be based upon what the owner told you, and one's opinion of his truthfulness. Often post mortem would reveal only a few small pericardial haemorrhages, which in themselves are not necessarily diagnostic, but they could have been due to electrocution.

One case which springs to mind was the death of a young heifer belonging to Sam Clowes. It was a day during the summer when Sam was intent on finishing a roof repair job on the ridge of his farmhouse roof. The sky had become increasingly

A third successive ovine caesarean one Sunday afternoon.

ominous; Sam worked on to try and complete the job before the anticipated deluge.

There came a flash, followed immediately by a mighty crash of thunder. Sam clung tight to

THESE TWO PAGES

Smallholders Percy and Ellen Goodall, at Horton.

Percy

Tarring the roofs.

Son, Arthur, on tractor

the ridge; at least he was still alive. As he looked round he saw a cloud of smoke, (he thought), actually it was a cloud of steam, arising from a hedge fifty yards away. Then he saw his heifer stagger, collapse and die.

It was time to come down from the roof, so he did, and telephoned me. Arriving I heard the tale as we walked across to the hawthorn hedge. At its base was a crater, six inches wide and about a foot deep where the lightning had struck, instantly turning the water in the soil to steam, which Sam had seen. The heifer lay about four yards from the hedge.

Next day, on post mortem there was not a single sign to suggest the cause of death. In my report I stressed that fact, but went on to say that in the circumstances there was no doubt in my mind as to what had killed that heifer. Sam's insurance claim was successful.

I used to like going 'up the Hollins' at Horton. It was a track which ran up towards Biddulph Moor for a mile and a half from the village school - now the village hall. The track served the seven properties dotted along its length; all the farms were little ones.

At the top was David Edge who kept pigs. Below him was Horace Barnacle who had a small milking herd. Next was Edgar Edge; a huge man, very shy and a bachelor. He kept a few young cattle and was usually in his large vegetable garden. He would slowly raise a large hand as I drove past.

Below Edgars was Hollins farm where Arthur Corbishley lived. His farm was about the biggest; there were eight cows and a few young things. In addition he was gardener for Mr and Mrs Moxon of Horton Hall, grave digger and leader of the bell tower. One of his responsibilities was the ringing out of the old year and the ringing in of the new. This was an occasion of some ceremony. He would leave home about 11pm armed with a bottle of sherry and sufficient glasses to meet his team of ringers. After refreshment, they would ring the changes until the church clock

Dairy tuition at Park House Farm, Horton. The Holdcrofts from Park House are either side of the machine.
Ellen Sims, later Goodall, is on the right.

struck midnight, then, after a pause of some 5 seconds, Arthur himself would start to pull on the largest bell to sound a dong for every year of the present century. It was in the 1990s when I heard this tale. Arthur used to worry over losing count but I never heard that he did.

Below Arthur was Alan Heath and his wife and opposite him lived Johnny and Katie Clews brother and sister. Johnny milked two or three cows and had been a horseman to Colonel Nicholson in the old days. He still had old photos of the shire horses which had been his pride and joy. Katy had kept company with Edgar for years but nothing came of it.

Alan reared young cattle and fostered owl chicks and fox cubs. In addition he did some dealing in antiques, particularly sporting books. There was always something interesting to look at. He also kept bees. I remember his sycamore honey and heather honey fondly.

On Horton Bank lived Percy Goodall and his wife. I remember him up a ladder clipping his hedges when he was about 90. They were typical small farmers, keeping some poultry, a couple of cows and a few calves which they would be very proud of. He was embarrassed when there

Percy Goodall on stack

was only about a gallon of milk in the milk churn when the cows were going dry and said so to the lorry driver when he came to pick it up. Bob Heathcote was one of the last churn lorry drivers. He replied 'Eh, Mr Goodall there's people in Manchester depending on that milk!'

In the early '60s amongst our clients was a certain hill farmer. Ken was over sixty and had a bad chest but he was a kind man; he and Mrs Wood had bought a blanket for us as a wedding present. He ran a dairy farm. In the yard were three shippons, holding a total of around twenty cows. Of all colours; mainly Shorthorns and Ayrshires, and a few Friesians, newly introduced. In those days; for our practice, that was quite a good sized herd. He also kept a Shorthorn bull.

The farm, Mount Pleasant, in Elkstone, was on the edge of the moorlands, half way down a very steep hill. The house and the buildings were set in to the hillside, and the farmyard at the front looked out over the valley below. In those days Mount Pleasant used to sport a C.T.C. sign, (Cyclist's Touring Club). The farmhouse was stone built and had many rooms and as Ken and Mrs Wood had no children, there were several spare bedrooms. These, Mrs Wood filled every summer with a regular supply of visitors, who came mainly from Manchester, thirty five miles away. Many of the visitors came year after year. They came for the peace and quiet of the countryside, the novelty of living on a working farm, the views from the farmyard over miles of open country, and for Mrs Woods cooking, good, plain, and substantial. In addition to running the guest house during the summer, Mrs Wood was also in charge of the farm work.

Ken and Mrs Wood had a "lad" who helped them with the farm work; he was Charlie, who wasn't very big and wore a pair of corduroy breeches, a pair of clogs, and he too, was over sixty. Charlie was also a little deaf. Mrs Wood had a powerful voice; I can hear her bellow of "CHARLIE!" even now; when I think about it.

One day when I was visiting the farm, Ken told me the following tale. It seemed that one afternoon, the previous week, Ken had wanted to have a cow bulled; so he had asked Charlie to bring the bull out, on a staff. That meant that when the bull had done his job he could be put back in his stall with no bother. There was no bull pen, when the bull was not working he was tied up in the cow shed.

The cow was standing, ready, in the yard. Ken also thought that perhaps it would be as well if he cleared the farmyard of visitors, many of whom were lolling about in the sunshine in a somnolent state after an active morning exploring and a heavy lunch provided by Mrs Wood.

'I'll have to ask you to go indoors for a little while folks,' he announced. 'We are having the bull out to a cow." The visitors needed no second warning, they disappeared, like smoke.

However going indoors didn't mean that they were going to miss the fun; in no time at all the bedroom windows were being opened, one after the other; the openings filled with heads craning out to watch.

Charlie brought out the bull who was young and eager, a little over eager; for a time or two, he was so speedy in his approach, that despite Charlie's efforts to slow him down, he overshot his mark. However by the dint of Ken and Mrs Wood steadying the slightly apprehensive cow, and a little hard swearing from Charlie, the bull approached at only four miles a hour the next time, mounted, jumped, and his job was done.

As Charlie lead the bull back to his lair, Ken looked up and shouted to his visitors, 'Right folks, you can come down now.' While he was brushing up he became aware of a male visitor sidling up, a bit self conscious, towards him. 'No luck then?' said the visitor. 'How do you mean?' asked Ken, baffled. 'Well, I was watching,' said the visitor. 'You did your best; the bull, he did his best, but that cow, she wouldn't lie down, would she.'

At that, Ken doubled up, laughed, choked and wheezed then he wiped his eyes, and laughed and choked again. The tale made me laugh too.

Leek 1930s

Derby Street, Leek.

War Ag Event
Above (names of some present):
Bill Ratcliffe, Frank Buxton,
George Carr, George Goldstraw, George
Critchlow, Jim Sergeant

Left: David Harvey, Frank Buxton, Bill
Ratcliffe

Below: Frank driving a Cletrac crawler
tractor at Cheddleton Hospital Farm.
David Harvey was responsible for land
reclamation work.

Some of the people involved with the 'War Ag' outside their office at Pretty Polly factory, Buxton Road.

Ted Moult, celebrity guest at 1963 Leek Show.
Mrs Hancock, B. Biddulph, Alderman Hancock, Mr & Mrs Ted Moult, Mr & Mrs E. J. Hodgkinson (vet),
Mr & Mrs J. Sales, Roy Knight (auctioneer), and William, Tommy & Anna Moult in front

Farmers coach trip assembled outside
Biddulph & District Agricultural
Merchants in Bath Street.
c.1935

Brunt's Smithy in St Edwards Street.
Ron Allen is on the left, c 1940.

Garden Street c.1910.

The George Hotel, top of St Edwards Street opposite the Green Dragon (Swan)
and over the road from St Edwards Church

Davenports Mill 1953. Cyril Eardley, Department Manager, far left.

Paul Sales

My grandfather was William Wardle Sales. He lived at a big house in Ashbourne Road called Rosehaven, which he had built along with the mill called Progress Dyeworks. He was a tyrant and when he walked down Ashbourne Road or Derby Street, people would cross to the other side of the road not to meet him. A chap told me one day that his nickname was Blucher Sales. General Blucher was fighting Napoleon and he was a demon with long hair and a beard.

My great grandfather was a coal miner from Kingsley - down the pit with men under him. My father would say, 'When you've got men under you, you've got to be the boss.' That reflected in my grandfather and father. 'Because if you don't show them you are the boss they'll walk all over you!' Their attitude was that you did what you were told. We always had a good table and good clothes but I had too much discipline - very Victorian; now it's gone too much the other way.

My grandparents, father and uncles were all staunch Primitive Methodists; they followed Methodism after the Wesleys. Grandfather was a local preacher as well as being a tyrant. When I went along with my father to Mount Pleasant Chapel on a Sunday, my grandparents used to come in and sit at the front on the right-hand side, backs ramrod straight, two old style Victorians. It was a time when Methodism was beginning to change and they began to bless the offering. So when it came time to take the collection, a man took the plate first to my grandparents. They sat there with their arms folded and didn't give a penny. Father looked and said, 'Why aren't you putting any collection in?' Grandfather replied, 'They're not blessing my money!' He believed you gave money freely and in good faith and he didn't want it blessing. And many times I've witnessed if he didn't like the preacher or sermon, they'd get up and there was a great kerfuffle as they walked out of the chapel and slammed the door. They'd got their own ideas.

I went to Sunday school and had a good voice, a boy soprano. When it came to the Anniversary father said to me, 'Now my lad you've got this solo I want to hear you singing.' And he went to the back of the chapel, upstairs on the balcony and I had to sing so he could hear me, the hymn was 'Jesus Calling.'

They had the mill where they did silk dying, all by hand during the 1930s when it was hard to get a job. They were silk masters and were sticklers for matching - my father for all his faults was a master dyer, he could dye yarn very well. He worked very hard and was a tough man.

On Ashbourne Road in wartime father was away.When there were bombs dropping we went into the back lavatory, although there was an Anderson shelter in the field at the back. Grandfather owned the land off Springfield Road, where I learned to ride a bike. There were two ponds fed by a spring to feed Progress Dyeworks. When we were lads we used to go up there. There were three-spined sticklebacks and newts - speckled and long-tailed newts. We used to catch them.

When I came home from school I went to the mill with my bicycle. All the men wore clogs and it was steamy from the barques. Father would say, 'Right my lad there's four samples here to take out.' And he gave me the skeins to take. I had a little carrier bag on the back of my bike and the people he was dyeing the silk for wanted the various colours, it might be matt, flat or bright. I'd go down to Brosters to the man in the matching shop and if it matched he would write on the ticket 'passed' or 'too flat' or 'redye it again'. If I had samples for various mills and it came back 'passed' I was happy - and my dad was happy - but if they weren't..... Another place I went was Hills. There was an old man there who used to do the matching, William Hill. He had a mouthful of bad teeth and bad breath. You had to stand quite a few yards away from him.

When I was about to leave school father said to me, 'Here my lad, what are you for now?' I said,'I don't know.' And I didn't. He said, 'You can be an apprentice to a stonemason or go farm labouring.' I didn't want farming but I hadn't really got a choice. So at 16 I went to work at Tom Shukers at Bosley. I'd got the problem of getting from Leek to Bosley every morning so I was treated to a motorbike, mother lent me the money. It was £40 for a 2-stroke 197cc Ambassador. I had to sign an IOU for the money.

In March when I left school the roads were bad with snow all the way from Hugbridge to the farm up the Dumbers. One morning I got to the bottom of the Dumbers when the bike ran out of fuel so I pushed it up the road; intent on getting to work. Tom came out of the shed. He wore corduroy britches, gaiters and boots. 'Tha's late this morning Paul.' Bertha came out, 'Leave him alone, what's matter?' I said, 'I've run out of fuel.' I worked all day, to night time. Tom went to Leek but never offered to get any petrol. Sid Holland's garage was near Bosley crossroads so I had to push the bike out and free-wheel down the Dumbers and get there to put petrol in.

When I first went to the farm, one day he says to me, 'This cows bullin' in here.' Well I didn't know what that was. There was a bull in there and he said, 'We'd better get this cow out and have it served.' I thought, 'What's going to go on here?' We got her out and turned the bull out and I had to look away, I thought it was private - I didn't want to see, I was embarrassed.

He had a wooden thing like a little short ladder, two sides with 5 or 6 stays between, about 6 foot long. He put it behind a cow if it was calving - they were tied by the neck. He said 'I get calving on my own sometimes.' Well I'd never seen a cow calve, 'what does he mean' I thought. All I saw was the calves that were fed with buckets. So this piece of wood was to enable Tom to help the cow give birth. If it was lying down he could put a bar in with ropes onto the calf's legs and get a bit of leverage and as the calf was being born, keep moving the bar back.

My job was suckling the calves. One day Bertha was getting the milk ready and said, 'I'll have to go and make breakfast now.' So off she went after showing me what to do. So I fed them and as we sat round the breakfast table Tom said, 'An yer suckled them calves Paul?' I said 'Yeah.' 'What did yer do with that new dropped un?' I said 'I give it same as th'others.' 'Tha's WHAT? Tha'at 'ave that calf dayin'!' Bertha said 'Leave him alone Tom.' It had been used to milk and I'd given it suckling powder and Tom told me it was going to die. That's how much I knew; if it hadn't been for Bertha, I'd have been very worried.

I used to clean the cows out with a barrow, take it out of the shed, push it up a ramp and tip it over the edge. Tom would go off to Leek and leave me loading a rubber tyred tumbrill. When he came back from Leek he'd say, 'What an yer bin doin' Paul; an yer loaded tumbrill up?' 'Yes, I've done that and brushed the yard up.' Tom Shuker's yard was quite amazing, it was a rough stony yard but where the cows came out of the shed he'd got a line of hurdles down the side about 4 foot away from the shed doors and when the cows came out they couldn't walk all over the yard, they had to go down this 'alley' before they went into the field. Tom never had a speck of muck on his yard and if a cow did its mess I had to get a bucket of water and brush and clean it all up.

So he took the tumbrill and tractor off into the field and I used to follow with a muck rake - a long handled tool with a curved fork at the top. I took the backboard off the tumbrill and the muck 'ud start falling out and I raked a pile out and then he said, 'When you've got a decent pile Paul, put the fork up in the air and then I'll move on.' So without any words the signal was, get a pile out, put the fork up in the air and he'd move on. 'Now do seven strides.' So I methodically did seven strides, stop again, then put the muck fork up. When the muck got close to the front you had to lift the tumbrill, there was like a sword fitting and it tipped the trailer a bit, no hydraulics, it was all done manually so the muck floor would be sloping.

One day he said, 'Come on Paul, we'n goo down't field and I'll show you how't spread muck wi' a fork. You can get on't knockin' job.' He carried his fork under his arm and I'd got a fork with very short tines - they'd worn down with work. So Tom went to the first pile of muck and he'd start casting this muck out - he got low down in a crouching position. Some of it broke up as he threw it; of course it was second nature to anyone used

And above, Chairman's Sunday 1963, seen here at Mount Pleasant Methodist Church. John Sales, Chairman of Leek Urban District Council.

to it but I said, 'What must I do now?' He replied, 'You can knock lumps.' So I got the fork and had to tickle these lumps out so that it was all finely dressed and we did that all over the field. It was all spread by hand and knocked by hand and then chain harrowed in the spring and eventually rolled but I'd left him by then.

He said to me another day, 'We're goin' drainin' Paul.' He'd got a draining tool which is a narrow type of spade. I used to wear clogs, dad wore clogs in the dyeworks and I wore clogs when farming. People in Derby Street used to say, 'Ay Up, Sales is comin' again.' I was following a family tradition. So Tom showed me what to do. He took the clod off and put it on one side. There was a foot of topsoil then we'd get into the subsoil - go down a good 'graft' then put pipes in.

I was working there all day and when I went into the cowshed at night, brushing the muck out, my right foot was wet. I couldn't weigh it up but I'd worked that hard, the draining tool had worn a hole through the wooden floor of the clog. When I got home, I said to me dad, 'Look how hard I've been working with the draining tool.' He got me a new pair of clogs; they were about £2 then, and put some strips of steel underneath them.

I was there for 3 months and then went to Fred Alcock's at Lower Foker, milking by hand. I

Bailiffs House, Tittesworth Dam

Wardle Barn

didn't know how to but had to learn; my hands were so tired that I couldn't use the twist grips on the motor bike. There were 12 cows and I sat on a stool to milk them. After a few months I left there and went to Fred Biddulph's at Gawsworth where I lived in and came home at weekends. It was nice there. At Tom Shukers, I earned £1 10s a week for 47 hours but at Biddulphs I earned £3 a week.

Paul Sales with seed fiddle

Then father decided to buy a farm; it might have been to keep me out of the army. Upper Foker was part of the Abbey Estate. He went to the sale and started bidding; he'd taken the tenant, Isaac Bailey with him and when it got to £3500 for nearly 200 acres and Harry Goodwin, one of his council mates was bidding, father got Isaac to bid. When it got to £4000 father stood up in the saleroom and said, 'Gentlemen, are you aware that the tenant is bidding?' He

Abbey Farm

wasn't, he was bidding for father. So it was knocked down to Isaac Bailey and father gave him £50.

After a while they had a sale and I came and started on the farm, but I didn't know anything about farming; I didn't know a good cow from a bad one. Today if you had a son, you wouldn't dare put him on a farm with no knowledge of cattle or land or anything.

It was June 1957; there was a chap helping who used work for old Isaac. I said, 'I've got cut this field.' We'd got a mower off John West, a 7RTC Bamford land drive which cost £47 and an old tractor. So we cut this field and then it rained. Several days later and I didn't know what to do with this grass but I pretended I did. I said to this chap, 'It's raining, what shall we do?' He said, 'You'll have go and stand it all up again!'

I had to find out by hook and by crook; I didn't know you turned it and tedded it so then I got a side-delivery rake. It was a horse-drawn one converted to tractor, a Lister Blackstone. It could turn the grass or with a piece fitted in the middle, it could side rake for rowing up. That was before the Bamfords Acrobat came out.

We got the grass tedded out then it rained again. We had to buy a Nicholson tedder - a land drive again with steel wheels. We kept going through this stuff; the machine would put it over the top or kick it out. The weather brightened up and we got the hay loose. So then we had to have a hay loader; that cost £30 from Sid Holland's at Macclesfield. It was a green crop loader; we used row up then put this loader behind the trailer and collect it up - then unload it loose. That was before we started baling; George Howson baled for us, 6d a bale, it made such a difference. It was 4d when he first came, to get the business. Him and Sid Weston - they had Fordson Majors and Jones Balers. Of course today nobody even wants to handle small bales.

Now as I reflect over those rough, hard years, I thank God for his Goodness and Mercy in guiding me through life's labyrinth and letting me see how fortunate I am in having so much from so little to start with.

AND A FEW MORE RAILWAY PICTURES OF LEEK

Cheap Rail Trips from Leek

EARLY MORNING RETURN
FARE TO STOKE ... 1/10
Available by the 6.53 a.m.
and 7.57 a.m. trains
Weekly Season Ticket to
Stoke 12/3

EACH WEDNESDAY, SATURDAY
AND SUNDAY
To:
ALTON TOWERS ... 1/9
Weekdays depart 1.23 p.m.
Sundays depart 1.38 p.m.

ALL-IN-HOLIDAYS IN
SCOTLAND
All-in-holidays in Scotland from
£14 14s. 0d., children under 14
accompanying adults £10 10s. 0d.
inclusive of travel tickets, guaran-
teed seat on trains, accommoda-
tion, meals on train, gratuities.
For illustrated folder or handbill
apply to stations, offices or ticket
agencies.

Full details of these and other
excursions and cheap fare
facilities obtainable from stations,
offices and agencies.

BRITISH RAILWAYS

Leekbrook 1955
Courtesy J. Morten

Leek

Leekbrook Junction 1952
Courtesy J. Morten

Leek

Leek

Live fish delivery at Leek
Station late 1940s.